AF478391

Political Parties and Elections in the United States

José Martí

Political Parties and Elections in the United States

Edited, with introduction and notes, by Philip S. Foner

Translated by Elinor Randall

Temple University Press
Philadelphia

ISBN 0-87722-604-0
CIP on file
Translated by: Elinor Randall
Designed by: Umberto Peña

Published 1989 by Temple University Press, Philadelphia

Contents

Preface   vii

Introduction by Philip S. Foner   3

LETTER FROM NEW YORK, November 12, 1881   19

MARTI'S LETTERS, February 21, 1883   33

POLITICAL AFFILIATION, October 20, 1884   41

MARTI'S LETTERS, March 15, 1885   53

MARTI'S LETTERS, October 3, 1886   87

THE UNITED STATES, December 8, 1886   99

ELECTIONS! November 2, 1888   113

INAUGURATION, March 5, 1889   133

PREFACE

José Martí, the Cuban revolutionary poet, educator, writer of children's stories, art and literary critic, and journalist, was born in Havana, Cuba to lower middle-class parents on January 28, 1885.[1] Martí was only fourteen years old when Cuba's first war for independence against Spain broke out in 1868.[2] He immediately supported the war, and his commitment to this cause landed him, while still in adolescence, first in prison and later into exile. Nearly three decades of Martí's life—from 1881 to 1895—were spent in the United States.

In 1881, partly to shore up his precarious finances, Martí began to write what became his "Escenas norteamericanas" (North American scenes), also known as "En los Estados Unidos" (In the United States), for *La Opinión Nacional* of Caracas, Venezuela. However, the majority of his "Escenas" appeared, over a space of ten years, in *La Nación* of Buenos Aires, Argentina, then a leading Spanish-language newspaper, and in *El Partido Liberal* of Mexico City. They were also syndicated in most of Latin America's major newspapers. These articles are masterly chronicles and essays on life in the United States. They made Martí the most widely read journalist of his time in the Spanish language.

Martí's steady stream of articles in superb Spanish gave Latin Americans a familiarity with the United States "as it was never known before."[3] In the *Journal of Inter-American Studies* of April,

1963, Richard B. Gray observed of Martí's writings on the United States:

> If this work were as well known as that of Baron Alexis de Toqueville's *Democracy in America,* and Lord Bryce's *American Commonwealth,* his significance to the United States would place him above these other writers. For with consummate skill and sensitivity, Martí probed the depths of social, economic and political change in the United States in the last two decades of the nineteenth century, and evaluated its strengths and weaknesses with rare understanding.

Martí's views of the United States were influenced by both his personal observations and experiences and his thorough study of contemporary social critics in the United States. His own commentaries, however, surpassed nearly all of them in insight and sharpness.

Martí's newsletters covered every aspect of American life. There were descriptions of Coney Island in summer, a commencement in a girl's school, agricultural exhibitions, prize fights, the opening of the Brooklyn Bridge, the installation of the Statue of Liberty, the memorial meeting in honor of Karl Marx, Christmas and New Year's in New York, the publication of new books, murder cases and trials, the Negro and Chinese questions, the plight of the Indians, trade union and labor strikes, women's suffrage, political conventions, election campaigns, and the conditions and voting habits of European immigrants. With his deftly drawn portraits, he introduced his Latin American readers to such writers and thinkers as Emerson, Whitman, Whittier, Longfellow, Mark Twain, Louisa May Alcott, George Bancroft, and Washington Irving; to such social reformers as Wendell Phillips, Henry Ward Beecher, Peter Cooper, Henry George, and Father Edward McGlynn; and to such political figures as Grant, Garfield, Blaine, Tilden, Cleveland, Benjamin Harrison, and many others. Many of these biographical essays are among his masterpieces, including those about Emerson, whom he deeply admired because of his complete independence of mind; Whitman, whom he regarded as a "natural" poet belonging to no school and an exponent of "the poetry of liberty"; Wendell Phillips, of whom he wrote: "The whole universe took the form of a Negro slave in his eye," and "He was implacable and fiery, as are all tender men who love justice"; Peter Cooper, of whom he said: "He puts into practice the human Gospel," and Mark Twain, whose *A Connecticut Yankee in King Arthur's Court* he described as a "fight, cowboy style, with a lasso and gun" against oppression and poverty.

Over the years, Martí produced a series of intelligent critiques of U. S. society. These are not mere journalistic impressions, but are rich in analysis. Martí showed that he was not only an articulate synthesizer of descriptive details, but also adept at understanding the change that was taking place in U. S. society in the decade and a half between 1880 and 1895—the stratification of economic classes, the alienation of American workers, the transformation of competitive into monopoly capitalism, its impact on the emergence of U. S. imperialism, and the danger this posed for Latin America. His "Escenas norteamericanas" clearly show his dread of the steady advance of United States imperialism as it prepared to launch a campaign to conquer Latin America both economically and politically—with Martí's beloved Cuba as its first victim. Martí's writings helped alert Latin America to this danger.[4]

As Roberto Fernández Retamar, president of the Casa de las Americas and brilliant commentator on José Martí, has written: "It is important to bear in mind that, although Martí was endowed with literary greatness, he was above all a political creature in the fullest and most elevated sense of this so-called despised word."[5]

The ten articles by Martí published in the present volume are presented in chronological order. Two of the articles ("Letter from New York," November 12, 1881 and "Martí's letters," February 21, 1883) are a part of the dispatch sent by Martí from New York. The missing sections do not deal with the election and are not included. The selected articles fully substantiate Richard B. Gray's judgment that Martí probed the depths of political life in the United States "with consummate skill and sensitivity."

PHILIP S. FONER

Professor Emeritus of History
Lincoln University, Pennsylvania

NOTES TO PREFACE

1. There are three biographies of José Martí in English: Jorge Mañach, *Marti, Apostle of Freedom* (translation by Coley Taylor of *Marti, el Apóstol* (1944) (New York, 1950); Richard Butler Gray, *José Martí, Cuban Patriot* (Gainesville, Fla., 1962), and Félix Lizaso, *Marti, Martyr of Cuban Independence* (translation by Esther Elise Shuler of *Marti, místico del deber* (Westport, Conn., 1974). None of these studies, however, are based on the recent revisionist historiography that seeks to demystify Martí. John M. Kirk's *José Martí: Mentor of the Cuban Nation* (Tampa, Fla., 1983), is based on such research, but it is not a biography of Martí. There is need for a biography which incorporates the excellent scholarship on Martí recently published in Cuba and other Latin American countries, the United States, Canada, and England, as well as unpublished studies in the form of Masters' and Doctoral dissertations, in these countries.

2. For a study of the first and second wars for Cuban independence from Spain, *see* Philip S. Foner, *A History of Cuba and its Relations with the United States*, 2 vols. (New York, 1962-1963), and *The Spanish-Cuban-American War and the Birth of American Imperialism, 1895-1902*, 2 vols. (New York, 1972).

3. Sturgis E. Leavitt in preface to Manuel Pedro González, *José Martí: Epic Chronicler of the United States in the Eighties* (Chapel Hill, North Carolina, 1953), p. viii.

4. On U. S. expansion, *see* Philip S. Foner and Richard C. Winchester, editors, *The Anti-Imperialist Reader*, Vols. 1 and 2 (New York, 1982-1983), and Lloyd C. Gardiner, Walter La Feber and Theodore McCormick, *Creation of the Modern American Empire—U. S. Diplomatic History* (London, 1973).

5. Roberto Fernández Retamar, "The Modernity of José Martí," in *José Martí: Revolutionary Democrat*, edited by Christopher Abel and Nissa Torrents (London and Durham, North Carolina, 1968), p. 2.

Political Parties and Elections in the United States

INTRODUCTION

BY PHILIP S. FONER

In 1880, at the beginning of his long stay in New York, Martí was immediately attracted and even dazzled by its democratic institutions, its creative power, and the opportunity it provided for every kind of individual initiative. To a person coming from Spain, with its decadent monarchy, or from Cuba or some of the Latin American republics, with their feudal societies, social castes, clerical hierarchies, and artificial inequalities, North American democracy seemed like a Promised Land. In his chronicle "Impressions of America," written on July 10, 1880, Martí exulted: "I am, at last, in a country where everyone seems to be his own master. . . . One can be proud of the species. Everyone works; everyone reads." And again: "I am deeply obliged to this country where the friendless find always a friend and a kind hand is always found by those who look honestly for work. A good idea finds always here a suitable, soft, grateful ground. You must be intelligent, that is all. Give something useful. You will have all what you want. Doors are shut for those who are dull and lazy; life is sure to those who are faithful to the law of work."

Yet in the same "Impressions," Martí called attention to what was already becoming a shortcoming in this country when he emphasized the need for spiritual development as well as commercial activity. He warned of the danger to the United States if the former languished while the latter flourished. "If this love of richness is not tempered and dignified by the ardent love of intellectual pleasures. . . ," he asked, "where shall they go. . . ?"[1] It was a warning Martí was to sound on many occasions. "I know," he wrote in *La Nación* of May 9, 1885, "that a nation which fails to cultivate the arts of the spirit, coupled with those of commerce, becomes fat as a bull, and will overflow its own temples, like a spilling of decomposed entrails, when its resources are exhausted."[2]

Gradually, the bitter reality of many aspects of life in the United States cleared away the mist from Martí's eyes, and he observed the discrepancies and contradictions in the scene around him. Martí had arrived in the midst of a radical transformation in the country's economic and social life, and he was quick to realize that his concept of the United States as a land where social distinctions were being obliterated and where the poor had equal opportunities with the rich to enjoy the fruits of democracy, was in drastic need of revision.

The 1880s were characterized by the rapid growth of American industry, accompanied by a tremendous concentration of capital and the appearance of giant corporations. With the rise of industrial trusts, like the Standard Oil Company, and huge banking houses such as J. P. Morgan & Co., monopoly became the dominant feature of U. S. capitalism. The age of the small manufacturer and of free competitive enterprise was passing. It was being replaced by what was widely called in the eighties "The New Feudalism." Said President Grover Cleveland in a message to Congress on December 3, 1886: "As we view the achievements of aggregated capital, we discover the existence of trusts, combinations, and monopolies, while the citizen is struggling far in the rear or is trampled to death beneath an iron heel. Corporations which should be carefully restrained creatures of the law and servants of the people, are fast becoming the people's masters."

"There are too many millionaires and too many paupers," declared the *Hartford Courant* in 1883. All of the United States was a land of contrasts, of gnawing poverty amidst enormous wealth. The "robber barons" who made up the new plutocracy vied with each other in "conspicuous waste." At the other end of the scale, the workers, earning between fifty cents and one dollar for a working day of ten to twelve hours, were unable to obtain the bare necessities of life.

The masters of banking, industry, and commerce were also the masters of the country's political life. The pernicious influence of

4

big business in all branches of government—executive, legislative, and judicial—had already been noted by Mark Twain in *The Gilded Age,* which he published in collaboration with Charles Dudley Warner in 1873. It was in the 1880s, however, that it reached such scandalous proportions that scarcely a week went by without some public disclosure of illegal concessions being granted to corporations, passed into law by bribed legislators, signed by corrupt executives, and approved by judges who were tools of the corporate interests.

The 1880s were also years of great workers' struggles. In cities and towns throughout the land, the armies of labor organized and gave vent to the pent-up bitterness of years of exploitation in a series of strikes that shook the nation to its foundations. Never before had the United States witnessed labor struggles of such vigor and scope.[3]

As he witnessed these developments, Martí's attitude toward the United States underwent a transformation. While praising many of its great men and acknowledging the virtues of its people, he increasingly pointed out the negative features of U. S. society in his dispatches. In May, 1882, the editor of *La Opinión Nacional* informed Martí that a number of his articles had not been published and asked him "to abstain in his criticism from bitter remarks on the vices and habits of that people [North Americans]."[4] Martí's response was to stop writing for the newspaper. A few months later, he sent his first article to *La Nación* of Buenos Aires. This article was mutilated by the editor, who wrote to Martí on September 26, 1882:

> Without denying the truth and sincerity of your views, we have deemed it necessary, given the extremely radical form of their conclusions, to remove part of your article. This is because your article differs to some extent from the lines of policy that we have established and which should be followed in the new and important service of foreign correspondents that we have just stated.
>
> The suppressed part of your article, although containing considerable truths, could lead our readers into the error of believing that we were opening a campaign of denunciation against the United States as a body politic, as a social entity, as an economic center. . . . Your article would have been all darkness, if it had been published as it went. . . .[5]

"Thus," Roberto Fernández Retamar points out, "Martí confronted a bitter dilemma as he began elaborating his critique of U. S. society: either to lose a forum that had resonance throughout the Hispanic world, or to proceed in an indirect manner. Naturally, he opted for the second."[6]

Martí was forced to become more subtle in his discussion of the United States. Nevertheless, his criticism continued. In September, 1883, he compared the gaiety of Coney Island with the poverty and squalor of New York slums, where "the children of the poor are dying by the hundreds as the summer progresses," where "the *cholera infantum* is sucking away the children's lives. A boa constrictor would leave the children of the poor in no worse condition than they are left by New York's summer—withered, wasted, cadaverous, all skins and bones." He angrily called this condition of the "poor children" "a national crime, and that abolishing this unnecessary misery is an obligation of the state."[7]

The more Martí came to know United States society, the better he was able to grasp the bitter realities of what lay behind the facade. He ceaselessly exposed and attacked the living and working conditions of the urban workers. Thus he wrote:

> We are at the height of a capitalist and labor struggle. For the first-named there is credit in the bank, there are prospects from the creditors, the seller's installments plans, the year's end accounts. For the worker there is a daily reckoning, the urgent and undeferable need, there are the wife and child who eat in the evening what the poor man worked for in the morning. And the well-to-do capitalist compels the poor worker to labor for a miserable wage.[8]

As he noted that "the national government has been slipping out of the citizens' hands," Martí recoiled with revulsion and anger from the practices which had reduced the electoral process in the United States to "an open market, where honor is bought and sold in back rooms"[9] (He detested James G. Blaine, the corrupt Republican Senator from Maine and presidential candidate, to whom he referred as "marketable Blaine," a politician who sold himself to the highest bidder).[10] Martí described "all-embracing bosses who control the parties in every city,"[11] the "petty head of the party, the one who prepares the elections, twists them, profits from them, gives votes to his friends, denies them to his enemies, sells them to his opponents."[12] He described how "Democratic ballots were substituted for Republican ones, or the latter were increased at will or the count was falsified," and how "in the States, money set aside for public expenditures disappeared into private purses."[13]

Speaking of Tammany Hall, the Democratic Party's machine in New York City, headed by an all-powerful political boss, Martí wrote: "So it is that here, where everything depends on the vote, confronting Tammany Hall is like signing one's own death warrant."[14] Martí insisted that men who were elected or appointed by political bosses "cannot be honest representatives. Such slaves cannot be men charged with defending freedom."[15]

Martí paid tribute to the Republican Party in its early years after its birth in 1854 as a coalition against the further extension of slavery, especially during the administration of Abraham Lincoln, the first Republican president, elected in 1860 on the eve of the Civil War. He revered Lincoln for having signed the Emancipation Proclamation during the war, which freed all slaves in areas of the South still in rebellion against the government of the United States.[16] He noted, however, that after the Civil War and Lincoln's assassination, the Republican Party became the corrupt tool of party bosses and corporations. Decomposition began immediately: "The manifesto of human liberty turned into a house of usury." The nation was turned into "a banquet and the fat, successful Republicans were permanently seated at the table."[17] From 1860 to 1884, the Republican Party dominated the presidency, both houses of Congress, and the Supreme Court and most of the state legislatures and executives in the North.

"The monopoly," Martí wrote, "sits like an implacable giant at the door of all the poor."[18] He castigated the Republican Party for hastening the rise of monopolies through its protective tariff legislation. Such protectionism raised prices so that the great masses could not buy "at a fair price the necessities of life," and monopolists "imposed upon the nation their inferior products at higher prices." These protected industries were "the very flesh of the Republican Party."[19] The workers, on the other hand, were unable to buy back the goods they produced, while the "surplus goods of this monopoly capitalist economy were too expensive to export."[20] The result was that the economy plummeted and a depression began in 1882 that lasted until 1886. At the depths of this depressed period in 1884 there were close to a million unemployed workers in the U. S. Factories were closed and wages were reduced.

Martí made it clear that behind the politicians were the financial and industrial magnates who exercised the power to select the candidates of both parties. "Elections," Martí wrote in *La Nación* of August 15, 1886, "are quite costly. The capitalists and large companies help the needy candidates with their campaign expenses; once the candidates are elected, they pay with their slavish vote for the money which the capitalists lay out in advance."[21] While the capitalists generally favored the Republican candidates, they were actually non-partisan. Martí wrote of "capitalists who, in exchange for laws that are favorable to their undertakings, support the party that offers those laws."[22]

Martí was the first to reveal to the people of Latin America the methods employed by the great corporations and monopolies of the United States in exercising their control over the country's political institutions. He was also the first to reveal the corruption and immorality in government that flowed from this domination of big business over the nation's politics.

"A United States Presidential campaign is rough and nauseating," Martí wrote in *La Nación*.[23] This process began at the conventions, where the presidential candidates were nominated in an atmosphere of corruption, behind-the-scenes manipulation, and the buying and selling of delegates' votes. He continued:

> Once the candidates are nominated in the conventions, the mire rises to the saddle pommels. . . . Pails of mud are dumped upon heads. Lies and exaggerations are knowingly spread. Bellies and backs are polished. All manner of infamy is considered legitimate. All kinds of blows are good as long as they stun the enemy. Whoever invents an effective villainous act struts about like a peacock. Even prominent men believe themselves excused from the more trivial duties of honor.[24]

Jorge Ibarra, a Cuban authority on Martí, points to Martí's conviction that "U. S. democracy would be nothing but fraudulent while the large monopolists rule the country."[25] Martí was not confident that this condition would soon end, and he asked:

> What has the Senate done to stop these evils, the Senate where the millionaires, the large landowners, the railway magnates, the mining tycoons, form the majority, despite the fact that senators are chosen by the state legislatures elected directly by the people who do not own the mines, the land or the railways? . . . . Although the country votes for it directly, the House of Representatives is chosen by such corrupt methods that every election is falsified by the use of vast sums of money. Has a single voice been raised in the House of Representatives to denounce the danger and to speak for the needy?[26]

Skeptical though he was that reform of the corrupt political system would ever take place—"once the rot sets in, the social body can rarely recover"[27] — he saw some hope in the fact that honest Republicans and Democrats were united in the demand to reform the manner in which candidates were chosen and elected, to amend or abolish the tariff laws, and to end the power of corporations over the political process.[28] However, he was deeply disappointed with Republican President Chester A. Arthur, who succeeded James A. Garfield to the presidency after the latter's assassination and was himself a product of the corrupt political system. Despite his pledge to do so, Arthur was unable to produce any important reform in the system. Martí, however, still had hopes that Grover Cleveland, the Democratic president elected in 1884 after a bitter contest against James G. Blaine, would bring the much-needed reforms. Cleveland had been a reform mayor of Buffalo, New York and a reform governor of New York State, and he ran for president on a reform platform. To be sure, Martí saw the triumph of Cleveland at the Democratic presidential convention as a victory for "the politicians, with their obese bellies and shaven heads, the smart politicians, who know where the votes are and how to manipulate them. . . ."[29] Nevertheless, he still expressed the hope that Cleveland would put his reform program across.

It was not to be. Martí wrote bitterly:

> And it turns out that after two years of enjoying power, with the executive in its hands, and with a majority in the House of Representatives, the Democratic Party has not reformed the tariff, has not honestly discussed the silver question, has not reduced the hundred million dollar surplus

in the national treasury. . . . and has not truly legislated with a spirit different from that of the Republicans.[30]

Martí's last hope rested on his belief that the workers of the United States would bring about the necessary changes in the political system. "Profit creates worms," he wrote. "It is among the poor that the sincerity which drives the worms away prospers."[31] His hope now centered on the United Labor Party, headed by Henry George, whose followers he described as "the most brilliant and conspicuous group of those attempting reform. . . . " The "Georgists" were "spreading the ideas of legitimate democracy of reform in present-day labor conditions, of transforming the land into public property, and uniting all contributions in one sole tax upon occupied land. . . . " He saw significance in the fact that "their doctrines are finding no reception in the powerful corporations which today are disposing of almost all productive wealth. . . . "[32]

The features of Henry George's theories that most attracted Martí were made clear in his review of *Progress and Poverty*, George's book published in 1879, which became one of the most widely read works on political economy in the United States. Martí wrote:

> In this book which examines the causes of growing poverty in spite of human progress, the essential idea is that the land must belong to the nation. From there the book derives all the essential reforms. He who improves the land should own it. . . . Nobody should pay the state taxes beyond the land rental. Thus the weight of national taxes would be on those that have received from the nation the means of paying them. . . . Life without taxes would be cheap and easy and the poor will have the means and time to cultivate their minds, understand their civic duties, and love their children.[33]

Unfortunately, the United Labor Party, which Henry George headed and which seemed to be flourishing after his narrow defeat in New York City's mayoralty election of 1886, fell apart because of internal conflicts, spurred in large measure by George's anti-Socialist prejudices.[34] Martí's hopes were again dashed. By the end of the decade, his last illusions about the United States had disappeared.[35] "Now we see close at hand what *La Nación* has seen for several years: the people's republic is being changed into a republic of classes;

10

the privileged, powerful, with their wealth, defy, exasperate, squeeze and expel from the free square of life those who come to it with nothing but their labor and intelligence; the rich are on one side and the poor on the other. . . . " So he wrote in the Spring of 1888.[36]

In 1983, Cuban vice-president and Martí scholar Carlos Rafael Rodríguez said of Martí's contemporary relevance: "His advice and example are so fruitful and his lesson so valid that we can consider him as the greatest among us, never distant, always at our side."[37] The modern day relevance of Martí to the United States becomes clear when we examine the contemporary political scene in this country. There have of course been improvements in U. S. politics since the 1880s. Conventions for the nomination of presidential candidates are still held, but direct primaries for the selection of the delegates to these conventions have reduced the power of political bosses and monopoly corporations. Reduced—but not eliminated them.[38] Although the Watergate investigation of the 1970s did not delve into the role of the giant corporations in political campaigns, it did disclose that on March 22, 1972, the political education section of the dairy industry (an organization created to contribute funds to candidates who would favor that industry) turned over $ 35,000 to the Committee for the Reelection of the President (CREEP) set up to reelect President Richard M. Nixon. This followed a meeting with the president himself. After the Secretary of Agriculture authorized an increase in the price of milk, CREEP received contributions from the dairy industry of over $ 400,000.[39]

Martí wrote contemptuously of the inauguration of Republican President Benjamin Harrison on March 1, 1887, during which there was a lavish display of wealth and finery.[40] However, this was nothing compared to the expenditures for the inauguration of Republican President Ronald Reagan on January 20, 1981, more than ninety years after the one described by Martí. The committee set up to organize the Reagan inauguration spent about eight million dollars on the event.[41]

The widespread use of television has been an important factor in bringing about the skyrocketing costs of political campaigns in the United States. Candidates have to raise many millions in order to be able to make their case on television, and it is virtually impossible for a poor, or even middle-class citizen to hope to be a successful candidate for high office. Indeed, many of the candidates for the presidency are compelled to abandon their campaigns during the primaries because they have run out of the funds they need to continue.

In May, 1987, the *Boston Globe* reported that candidates for Congress had spent $ 450 million in the 1986 campaigns. Its report read:

> WASHINGTON — House and Senate candidates spent a record $ 450 million in the 1986 elections, up 20 percent from 1984 and double what they spent just eight years ago, according to a government report released yesterday. The preliminary report by the Federal Election Commission on congressional receipts and expenditures for the two-year 1985-1988 election cycle showed that candidates for the 34 Senate seats raised $ 214 million and spent $ 211 million—an increase of 24 percent over 1984 spending. Candidates for the 435 House seats in 1986 raised $ 257 million and spent $ 239 million during the election cycle, a 24 percent increase from 1984, the commission said. . . . [42]

In that same month, *The New York Times* also reported:

> A private study estimates that spending on national, state and local political campaigns reached a new high of $ 1.8 billion in the last Presidential election year.
>
> The cost of elections in 1984 marked a 50 percent increase over that for the 1980 campaigns, according to Prof. Herbert Alexander of the University of Southern California, a political analyst, and Brian Haggerty, a researcher in a study for the Citizens' Research Foundation, a private group studying campaign finances. . . . [43]

Martí's warning to the people of the United States is full of meaning today during the era of Reaganism when, to use Martí's own words, no conditions exist "worthy of higher esteem than wealth."[44] He wrote:

> In this restless, sumptuous, and enormous nation life is no more than the conquest of wealth. This is the disease of this country's greatness. It has attacked the liver and invaded all one's entrails. It is upsetting, deforming, and disfiguring everything. The imitators of this great nation are careful not to contract this sickness.[45]

NOTES TO INTRODUCTION

1. *The Hour* (New York), July 10, 1880. José Martí, *Obras Completas* (Havana, 1975), XIX, pp. 103, 104. Hereafter cited as O. C.

2. *La Nación* (Buenos Aires), May 9, 1885. O. C., *X*, p. 184.

3. Philip S. Foner, *History of the Labor Movement in the United States,* II (New York, 1955), pp. 3-14; Eliot Jones, *The Trust Problem in the United States* (New York, 1921), pp. 20-22; *Hartford Courant*, reprinted in *John Swinton's Paper,* December 30, 1883; Charles E. Spahr, *An Essay on the Present Distribution of Wealth in the United States* (New York, 1896), p. 116.

4. Quoted in Retamar, *op. cit.,* pp. 8-9. The contents of this first article by Martí for *La Nación* are not known.

5. *Ibid.,* p. 9. Another example of the censorship Martí faced was in the case of the short-lived magazine *La Edad de Oro,* published in New York between July and October, 1889 and written expressly for "the children of America." Only four numbers of the journal appeared, after which there was a serious difference of opinion between Martí and the publisher (a wealthy Brazilian, A. D. Acosta Gómez), apparently over the religious content which the publisher wanted in the journal and which Martí refused to include. (John M. Kirk, "José Martí and his concept of the *intelectual comprometido,*" in Abel and Torrents, *op. cit.,* p. 116).

6. Retamar, *op. cit.,* p. 9.

7. *La Nación* (Buenos Aires), October 21, 1883. O. C., IX, pp. 458, 459.

8. *La Nación* (Buenos Aires), September 13, 1882. O. C., IX, p. 332.

9. *La Nación* (Buenos Aires), May 9, 1885. O. C., X, p. 193.

10. *Ibid.*, p. 199.

11. *La Opinión Nacional* (Caracas), November 26, 1881. O. C., IX, p. 107.

12. *La Opinion Nacional* (Caracas), November 15, 1881. O. C., IX, p. 97.

13. *La Nación* (Buenos Aires), May 9, 1885. O. C., X, p. 193.

14. *La Nación* (Buenos Aires), October 1, 1884, O. C., XIII, p. 277.

15. *La Nacion* (Buenos Aires), March 31, 1883. O. C., IX, pp. 358-359.

16. *Ibid.* In one of Martí's most famous statements, he wrote: "We love the country of Lincoln as much as we fear the country of Cutting." (José Martí, "A Vindication of Cuba," *New York Evening Post,* March 25, 1889). Francis Cutting was one of the leaders of the American Annexationist League which had designs on annexing Cuba to the United States. He also aroused the anger of Mexico by insulting the nation.

    When Martí was twelve years old, Abraham Lincoln was assassinated, and he joined in the mourning. "For two men I trembled and wept on learning of their death," he wrote later. One was Don José de la Luz Caballero and the other Abraham Lincoln. [*See* Emeterio S. Santovenia, *Lincoln in Marti: A Cuban View of Abraham Lincoln* (Chapel Hill, North Carolina, 1953), p. 4.]

17. *La Nación* (Buenos Aires), May 9, 1885. O. C., X, pp. 192, 197.

18. *La Nación* (Buenos Aires), October 26, 1884. O. C., X, p. 84. Retamar notes that the monopoly Martí refers to was not confined to industrial monopoly capitalism, but included also the beginnings of "the fusion of banking capital with industrial capital in a financial oligarchy," and that this was related to the emerging U. S. imperialism. He argues, therefore, that "Martí realized a pre-Leninist analysis of imperialism, even before imperialism displayed those mature features that Lenin diagnosed in his classic work, *Imperialism—the Highest Stage of Capitalism,* a popular outline, twenty-one years after Martí died. (*Op. cit.,* pp. 6-7.)

19. *La Nacion* (Buenos Aires), March 31, 1883. O. C., IX, p. 357.

20. Peter Turton, *José Martí: Architect of Cuba's Freedom* (London, 1986), p. 120.

21. *La Nación* (Buenos Aires), August 15, 1886. O. C., XI, p. 16.

22. *La Nación* (Buenos Aires), May 9, 1885. O. C., X, p. 190.

23. *Ibid.*, p. 185.

24. *Ibid.*

25. Jorge Ibarra, "Martí and Socialism," in Abel and Torrents, *op. cit.,* p. 90.

26. *Ibid.* Article I, Section 3 of the Constitution provided for the election of U. S. Senators by the state legislatures. With the adoption of the seventeenth amendment to the Constitution in 1913, Senators were elected by direct popular vote.

27. Jacqueline Kaye, "Martí in the United States: The Flight from Disorder," in Abel and Torrents, *op. cit.*, p. 75.

28. *La Nación* (Buenos Aires), May 9, 1885. O. C., X, p. 198.

29. *La Nación* (Buenos Aires), December 16, 1885. O. C., X, p. 346.

30. *La Nación* (Buenos Aires), January 26, 1887. O. C., XI, p. 120.

31. *Ibid.*, p. 123.

32. *Ibid.*, pp. 123, 124.

33. *La Nación* (Buenos Aires), April 14, 1887. O. C., XI, pp. 145-146. Jorge Ibarra points out that Martí was impressed by Henry George's theory also because it "sought to preserve the capitalist system in the United States by diverting the floating population of the cities and the mass immigration of the North American ports towards farming." (Ibarra, *op. cit.*, p. 97).

34. Foner, *History of the Labor Movement in the United States*, II, pp. 236-250.

35. Retamar, *op. cit.*, p. 8. Jorge Ibarra writes in this connection: "The years 1885-1887 are decisive in the ideological evolution of Martí. In 1885, Martí had complete trust in the popular vote, which he considered made the big difference between Europe and the United States. He had faith, too, in the representatives elected by the people and he believed that the democratic system ruling in the United States was the solution to all problems. But by 1887, he understood that such a system was a fraud." (Ibarra, *op. cit.*, p. 87.)

One should add that as the Haymarket Affair in Chicago unfolded, and the legal frameup of the eight anarchists and champions of the eight-our day became clear, Martí became more critical of democratic institutions in the United States. As Peter Turton observes: "Martí's faith in the United States had received a mortal blow in the Haymarket events, and later occurrences only served to confirm and deepen his rejection of that nation as a model." [*José Martí: Architect of Cuba's Freedom* (London, 1986), pp. 143-144.] For Martí's writings in English on the Haymarket Affair, *see* Philip S. Foner, editor, *Inside the Monster: Writings on the United States and American Imperialism*, translated by Elinor Randall (New York, 1973).

36. *La Nación* (Buenos Aires), May 17, 1888, O. C., XII, p. 425, reprinted in English in *José Martí Replies: Materials Referring to José Martí and the Radio Martí Project. Prepared and Compiled by the Center for Studies on José Martí* (Havana, 1982), p. 13.

37. Carlos Rafael Rodríguez, "Martí en el nuevo Ayacucho," in *Casa de Las Américas*, No. 138, May-June, 1983, p. 47. English translation by Roberto Fernández Retamar, in Retamar, *op. cit.*, p. 3.

38. William S. Domhoff, *Who Runs the United States?* (New York, 1970), pp. 142-145.

39. Víctor Alba, *Watergate* (Barcelona, Spain, 1975), p. 131; José A. Benítez, "The North American Presidential Elections," unpublished manuscript (Havana, 1987), pp. 13-14.

40. *La Nación* (Buenos Aires), December 11, 1888. O. C., XII, pp. 87-100, *see also La Nación* (Buenos Aires), April 16, 1889. O. C., XII, pp. 167-180.

41. *The New York Times.* January 22-23, 1981.

42. *Ibid.*, May 14, 1987.

43. *Ibid.*, May 31, 1987.

44. Ivan P. Boesky, when he was still the giant of the takeover profiteers and a model on how to get rich quickly (even if illegally), told a group of business students in 1985: "I think greed is healthy. You can be greedy and still feel good about yourself."(*The New York Times.* December 13, 1987.) This theme is carried over in greater detail in the motion picture *Wall Street,* where Michael Douglas, portraying corporate raider Gordon Gekko (modeled on Boesky), sums up the "morality" of a substantial section of the business community. "The point is, ladies and gentlemen," he tells a shareholder's meeting, "greed is good. Greed works, greed is right. Greed clarifies, cuts through, and captures the essence of the evolutionary spirit. Greed in all its forms, greed for life, money, love, knowledge, has marked the upward surge of mankind—and greed, mark my words—will save not only Teldar Paper [Company] but that other malfunctioning corporation called the U.S.A." (*Ibid.*, December 6, 1987.)

45. *La Nación* (Buenos Aires), July 16, 1884. O. C., X, p. 63. For the untenable view that Martí was uncritical of the United States, and that any other interpretation is simply the result of the imposition of a Marxist viewpoint, *see* Carlos Ripoll, *José Marti, the United States and the Marxist Interpretation of Cuban History* (New Brunswick and London, 1984).

LETTER FROM NEW YORK

LAZY PEOPLES. — HONEST ELECTIONS. — A MILLIONAIRE IS DEFEATED BY A WORKER. — AN ELECTORAL CAMPAIGN. — RESOURCES, HABITS, PREPARATIONS, EXTRAORDINARY EXPENSES, ELECTION DAY.

New York, November 12, 1881.

To the Editor of *La Opinión Nacional:*

These recent days in New York have been days of drama, of the anxiety of winning and losing, of splendor and surprise. Living in these times makes a person dizzy. Neither the pleasure of remembering nor the refreshing effect of rest are given to those who, in the marvellous regatta, have the need to look perpetually toward the future. Choked and covered with dust, blood-spattered, our guns unpolished or broken, we arrive at the way station, fall weakly to the ground, and leave to our beloved sons our dented armor, now tempered again in the heat of battle; and at the threshold of the house of death, our shattered helmets finally roll to the ground. The hasty, intoxicated, maddened fighters knock down, stamp upon, wound, tear to pieces, or, to clear the way, steal away whoever stops in the road, whether a man or a nation. And if still alive and repentant for his weakness, the fallen rises vainly to his feet, repairs his dented armor, and tries to move the rusted steel. Great fighters, persisting in the search of what is to be, have gone beyond the magnificent horizon. They go far, far indeed! And the lazy have been forgotten.

The able horseman must not relinquish the reins, nor must the free man give up his rights. It is certainly more comfortable to be led than to lead, but it is also more dangerous. And putting one's own self to use is a very splendid thing—very strengthening, invigorating, and ennobling. The people of this nation were beginning to forget these things, and inasmuch as buying and selling votes was a supreme law, an implacable master, and the origin of all power, the elegant gentlemen and mighty potentates found it less difficult to join forces for buying and selling votes than to join forces to vote honestly. There are elections here every year, but the ones held now have been like the arrogant and angry awakening of a strong man who knows he has been imposed upon while asleep.

19

Elections in New York, as throughout the Union, are of a special
kind, and in the most important, which are the Presidential, the
more obstinate, lordly or lazy elements go out to do battle, and
they fight with anguish, ferocity, rage, and all their will power and
strength. In the lesser "off-year" elections that are not Presidential,
certain efforts, certain measures which are more necessary for the
major struggle, are laid aside in order not to anger those elements.
The local parties, closely knit in the face of their closely knit rivals
in the great four-year struggle, subdivide and break ranks; personal
sympathies endanger the loyalty and discipline of the party sec-
tarians. Since one votes for men known intimately—family men
whose influence must be felt more in the home—they are doubted,
questioned, analyzed, taken apart, or loved even more. Emotions
take comical forms an instant after having been threatening. I'd
like to have the good city of Brooklyn go up in flames tonight, and
the good Low[1] with it!" said one of Low's defeated party members
as he stepped down from a carriage on election day. At the crack
of dawn a handsomely uniformed poor little messenger boy, a hard
worker for one so young—his eyes heavy with sleep, his hands
filled with telegrams to be delivered even as late as two in the
morning—returned to his poor little house to which he brings a
dollar a day, and which he leaves for his daily work again as soon
as the sun—which sees so many silent marvels—like a golden
Host, generator of life, rises in the sky. And when he was told, in
reference to the election: "But the poor love Seth Low, the mayor
elect," he replied: "Oh, no Sir; now we'll have to pay more rent;
he's a rich man and won't take care of the poor." "Well, Henry
Ward Beecher[2] says that few people love the poor as much as Low."
"I know as much about Henry Ward Beecher as anyone can in this
neighborhood," said the messenger boy with a serious expression.
"His wife once sent en errand boy to buy a penny's worth of milk,
gave him a two-cent coin and asked for change." And to a great
extent the childishness and self-assurance of that small boy reflect
the electoral struggle. Talmedge, an eloquent speaker although

1. Seth Low was elected Mayor of Brooklyn which was a separate city
   until 1900. He was elected as a reform Mayor.

2. Henry Ward Beecher (1817-1887) was a famous minister of the Plymouth
   Congregational Church in Brooklyn, New York (1847-1887), noted for
   his persistent fight against slavery. After the Civil War, he became
   increasingly anti-labor.

epileptic, in a recent religious talk rightly censured the ill turns, disloyalties, and voluntary omissions of the truth which become weapons with deliberate aim in the elections. The rival candidate is conspired against, ridiculed, disfigured, anathematized. But this time the elections did not have that local rancor or that lesser significance of the usual off-year contests, but that greatness of rebellion, and that singular virtue of vindications, and that beautiful energy with which betrayed men finally rise up against those who traffic with their decency and rights. The good spirit of Jefferson,[3] who ardently and majestically loved freedom, inspired the sluggish nation with courage. The practice of leaving the ballot boxes in the hands of drunken tramps and corrupt politicians, or of voting meekly for those candidates presented by the all-embracing bosses who control the parties in every city, has suddenly been replaced by the elimination of embarrassing pressures, and the correction of the fatal oversights which brought about the election of cowardly men who are creatures and slaves of the boss. The way has been barred to men whom the boss recommends for public office; and there has been an election, by energetic vote of a large majority, of some honest, useful, tested men—such as an excellent Mexican deputy— capable of giving up their high positions to their rivals, because they believed that the fervor of their friends or their party interests had brought to the election a conduct dissatisfying to a man of integrity. Faithless memory is now unable to recall the name of this good Mexican deputy. The mind ought to forget the base actions, and remember only the noble ones!

State and municipal elections have now been held, and they are important for arousing the nation to an awareness and a use of itself, and for breaking free from the hands of bold traffickers or arrogant bosses who were beginning to dispose of the people's vote as if it were their own personal wealth. There were many positions to be filled: State senators, representatives to Congress, high State positions: fiscal, engineering, and public treasury posts; and in Brooklyn, a Democratic city, a mayor was elected. Other States also held elections, but not as hard-fought or significant as those of noisy New York and domestic Brooklyn. In New York a strong,

3. Thomas Jefferson (1743-1826), author of the Declaration of independence, was elected third President of the United States in 1800, and served until 1809, having been reelected in 1804. He was one of the most learned and brilliant men in the history of the United States.

tight, extremely interesting contest would attract the eyes: a millionaire against a worker. In Brooklyn, apart from any minor characters who might lend amenity and brilliance to the contest, there was a stubborn struggle for electoral freedom. In New York a tall, imposing, slender, and elegant man named Astor[4] fought against a strong, broad-shouldered, simple, jovial, extremely modest man named Roswell Flower[5] for a seat in Congress. Brooklyn's mayor, who in his term of office has proved to be intelligent and honest, but who was soft wax in the hands of the formidable *boss*—the domineering chief of the city's political organization—presented himself for reelection against a young, charitable, fair-minded, impetuous rich man, the good Seth Low.

It is necessary, very necessary, to follow the contest of Flower and Astor. All contests are alike, but this one is more exciting, more vibrant and more of a reflection of the spirit and practice of this nation than any other political battle. Astor is a grand gentleman who has become a politician; he has palaces and yearnings for glory—which are other palaces—and in addition to his wealth he has the valuable gift of not looking upon his fortune as a right to idleness. He is poor in years but not in millions. He is a State Senator. But he is a member, and aspires to be a representative, of that singular aristocracy of fortune that in its quest for nobility tries to make people forget the only titles that honor it: its humble beginnings. Rich men of the first generation fondly recall those days when they were shop boys, stable boys, porters in woolen goods, firms, wretched errand boys, cowhands. But the second generation rich, who sprucely mount the horses which their parents led by the bridle, view as an escutcheon of indecorum in the newly rich that which for their parents was an escutcheon of honor: the self-made man. A well-to-do man in the process of accumulating his wealth is a base and contemptible being in the eyes of one who has already amassed his fortune. And there is a very deep abyss between the powerful by inheritance—thin, pale and resembling long flutes, as is the custom of English nobility, and those who have

4. William Waldorf Astor (1848-1919), wealthy son of John Jacob Astor, one of the richest men in the United States; entered politics as a Republican and elected to the New York State Assembly and Senate.

5. Roswell Pettibone Flower (1835-1899), New York broker and businessman; Democratic Congressman from New York (1881-1883 and 1889-1891), and New York governor (1892-1895).

attained power through work—healthy, chaste, determined, sturdy, and extremely clean with that old-time American cleanliness, which is sober and solid.

A political aristocracy was born from this monetary aristocracy, and it dominates newspapers, wins elections, and generally prevails in meetings over that overproud class that poorly disguises the impatience with which it awaits the time when the number of its partisans permits it to place a strong hand upon the sacred book of the motherland and to reform—for the favor and privilege of one class—the Magna Carta of generous freedoms under the protection of which these vulgar and powerful men created the fortunes they yearn to employ today in seriously undermining those freedoms. Astor supports and is supported by these men. The friends of what is here known in politics as a "strong government" are his friends. Stern Grant[6] and contemptuous Conkling[7] are defending him. For Astor it is a matter of a code of laws that his family, his millionaire family, must be represented in the Union's Congress, as in the ancient protection of the State in the ancient *Cortes*. And this was like an inopportune rehearsal of England's aristocratic system in which young nobles learn the art of government as an unavoidable duty and a compulsory right. Astor's opponent is a modest rich man of the first generation, who still keeps his brimless hat and worn-out shoes as trophies of victory. Today he rides in a carriage, but he says he went unshod for a long time. "I know the taste of that poor meal over which the working man bends so happily at noon, a meal brought from home in a tin pail," he used to say magnificently. Roswell Flower has the magnetism, the impulse, the appeal, and the power of attraction of new forces. Today he manages a bank where he is loved; in other days he held out his arms desperately in search of work. He tells the truth, scorns hypocrites, loves the unfortunate. He takes pride in his humility, which is the only wholesome kind of pride. His only weapon in his electoral campaign has been the

6. Ulysses Simpson Grant (1822-1885), eighteenth President of the United States. Honored for having helped save the Union in the Civil War, he brought to the presidency an incompetence which led to an administration noted for corruption and poor management even though he himself was personally honest and well-meaning.

7. Roscoe Conkling (1829-1888), lawyer and political boss of the New York Republicans, U. S. Senator from New York.

story of his life. "The working man will vote for me because I've been a worker. I walked about for many years, never seeing my feet without cuts and scars. Young men will vote for me because it will make them happy to see a man whose life shows them that from the humblest beginnings they can achieve the highest goals." Democrats and Republican opponents voted for him too. In the week before the elections, his district was something to see. VOTE FOR ASTOR appeared in black letters on big placards.

And ROSWELL FLOWER was seen in red, green, and blue letters on placards just as big. Posts, fences, piles of bricks, crumbling walls—all were plastered with very tall posters. Every hotel was the scene of a milling crowd, every beer hall a campaign headquarters. Carriages filled with campaign workers went up and down the streets of the district, and new people volunteered to work without pay for the Democratic candidate. Astor's campaign headquarters looked like a large telegraph office or the general staff tent of a military encampment. There was the incessant sound of envelopes being sealed, letters being folded, the scratching of pens. An outgoing messenger bumped into an incoming one. The district's voters and professional campaigners congregated like thirsty butterflies upon a honey-laden flower. And the services of every butterfly were weighted, calculated, and paid. One talked in low voices, entered by secret doors, shook hands mysteriously, smiled maliciously. Some people left sadly, as if feeling empty; others in a jolly mood as if loaded with a recent weight. Because the election of a representative to Congress costs the candidate or his party a minimum of $ 16,000, and Astor's campaign cost that wealthy warrior $ 80,000. He paid his clerks two hundred dollars a day. He mailed forty thousand circulars to his voters. Great cartloads of letters and circulars left the candidate's campaign headquarters. The electoral ward comprised one hundred and five districts of precincts, and each was given $ 100 to cover petty expenses. Out of the great number of volunteers—claiming to be influential among the voters—the useless were dismissed and the useful, because of their ability, skill, or influence, were regaled with $50 a day. When the millionaire passed by, the barrooms and beer halls turned into fountains of champagne, beer, and whiskey. The restless candidate went out early in the morning, although he was not used to such strolls or visits. His electoral ministry, composed of people adept at molding opinion and violating and enticing the public vote, accompanied him. Voracious reporters followed closely at his heels through the muddy streets in the pouring rain. They walked in his footsteps. Astor had merely to say a word or throw a coin upon the counter of a saloon to have these events immediately appear on the newspapers' copy desks. Reporters followed the rich young man like horseflies, and that war of horseflies has defeated him. It is to win sympathy, to mix with the voters, to dazzle them with a cordial phrase, a timely promise, an open manner or some pleasant conversation; it is to win favor with the saloon owners by generous gifts because they vote and induce others to vote, that candidates habitually visit the beer halls. The elections here have been heating up in those ovens. Upon those wooden counters there, the price of votes is offered, haggled over, and accepted; in a corner of those dark, smoke-filled rooms there, small groups of people talk mysteriously; the men who go about soliciting the popular vote there descend to trivial, tasteless jokes, unbecoming pleasures, and indecent familiarity; a candidate who is short of money there hints that loiterers who receive him with raucous laughter should order a modest drink, and says: "I wonder what these gentlemen want, a beer?" Another man there who is presently an ambassador in Europe, removes his coat in the absence of the bartendor, turns the bung of the barrel, serves beer to his guests, touches beer steins, shakes hands with the men, and wins them over with his graciousness and straightforwardness. The powerful Astor, with kid gloves, humble expression, and affable smile, entered the saloon. He invited the idle customers to champagne, no less, and to costly wines and excellent liqueurs. He tossed heavy twenty-dollar gold pieces upon the counter, accepting no change. The city has eighty breweries filled with voting workers, and he visited nearly all of them. The invited men drank up quickly, while the host barely lifted the beverage to his lips. He won the heart of a beer salesman because he spoke to him fluently in the language of his idolized *Vaterland;* but another German received him harshly, and another, after having emptied his pocket to buy some bad wine, turned down the vote solicited by the millionaire. The candidate went to a dance for the common people, and covered the counter with shiny coins with which he treated the dancers to drinks for some time, and danced with the most modest girls. In one place he defended one of his bills in the Senate, in another he apologized for having opposed some useful measures which he now vowed to support in Congress. Oh, how wretched the glory that reduces to such things and such practices those who yearn for its fleeting benefits! "I wouldn't give a cent to be elected!" said the honest Seth Low about this in Brooklyn, "nor will I treat others to the beer that I don't drink, nor will I buy votes that fail to do me honor." And Roswell Flower, Astor's opponent, did not engage in a "personal campaign" or a "beerhall campaign," as it is known in the city's political jargon. His tired voice refused to express any powerful thoughts, refused to tell his pure, crude, and honest phrases to the voters gathered in the meeting halls. He paused on the sidewalks; visited his friends; explained in this and that store, and to this and that group, the reasons for the present struggle and his conduct in the Congressional battles, in case he should succeed in being elected. Scores of voters went to his election headquarters to assure him that, in spite of having received heavy round coins from Astor's campaign workers, they would not give Astor their votes because he offended them by trying to buy them off; they would vote for him—for Flower. Astor's workers paid for a glass of Seltzer water with five-dollar gold pieces, and left the change for the proprietor "to entertain the boys when they come." And Roswell Flower turned down a group of Democratic workers who asked him for a small recompense; and to anyone who spoke to him about a possible purchase of some Republican votes, he bravely responded: "I don't expect my defeat, but I'd rather be defeated than owe my victory to the purchase of Republican votes. I want to keep my honor intact in this campaign." "My rival can defeat me, and he is surely far ahead of me in wealth and long legs, but my loyal Democratic voters will overcome that difference. I began my life as a poor boy of the people; the people will give me their votes, and so will the honest Republicans." The solemn day arrived. The election workers hovered around the small booths in which the ballot boxes, guarded by policemen, are customarily placed. And it is a well-known fact that the Republicans themselves—hurt by that business of buying men, and of shameful visitations to which the Republican candidate had descended—discarded from the pile the ballots bearing Astor's name, and went to the ballot boxes without them, or provided themselves with ballots bearing the name of Flower. At nightfall a sad young man, seated in the presidential chair at a broad table in an almost empty room, feverishly moved a nervous hand decorated with magnificent diamonds: it was Astor, surrounded by his humiliated lieutenants, who was receiving in letters and telegrams the news of his inglorious and sweeping defeat.

Flower defeated him by a majority of over two thousand votes in a district where in the previous election Astor's Republican followers had gotten the better of Flower's Democratic partisans by the same majority. It was a law that in a city of workers a worker should be elected. The future laws of a strong and upright nation are not at the bottom of a beer barrel, or in the base will of a few vagrants or needy dealers in votes. He who places his trust in corrupt men places it badly; for when the joy of money is over, in order to serve another master or to regain their self-respect, the corrupt, with a shrug of their shoulders, bring down the corrupters.

And the press, that new queen, that affable and powerful queen to whom Flower has given his warmest thanks, has been a weapon of death against the millionaire. It was not an insane hatred of wealth, but a virile repugnance of seeing it so basely employed. The educated newspapers complained and were angry about that attempted abuse of uneducated men. That method of buying men hurt their sense of decency. The young and the hopeful, the dreamers of glory, the journalists who watched the contest from near at hand, and wrote about it with cruel and implacable realism, were filled with rage against that spectacle which was preparing so despicable a cradle for laws, and so vile a use of liberties, and filling with such threats the future of a nation in which the keys to the house of laws can thus be bought and sold.

The chronicles of this campaign have been duelling rapiers, arrows, accusing tongues, piercing swords, and battle axes. This harsh and merciless lesson has come to the defeated millionaire from men's scorn and disregard, and this sensational beginning of the loss of power has come to the Republicans from the abuse of power in the State. "For if it's necessary to elect our representatives to Congress from among the young men of wealthy households," said one city newspaper abruptly and vigorously in response to another, "then how shall we have among us in the future such men as Henry Clay,[8] Abraham Lincoln,[9] and James Garfield?[10] For Garfield did not come from a wealthy family, his widowed mother planted hedges on country estates to earn the money to feed her children."

And those who have scourged the rich corruptor have kept in brilliant leadership, and raised in hymns of victory, a virtuous man of wealth: Seth Low, heir to the greatest fortune in Brooklyn, and mayor elect of that city by a landslide. He has been praised, defended, and congratulated. His supporters have engaged in an extremely lively campaign for him; Brooklynites have crowded into the meeting halls to hear that fine young man. He has been giving six to eight speeches every night, abounding in honest thinking, delivered slowly and in simple language—certainly not longwinded or punishing or meandering like Beecher's orations, but colloquial, calm and unadorned—more attentive to content than to style. Seth Low was elected by Republicans and Democrats alike because of their hatred of the political pressure being exerted in the city by a Democratic boss, and out of respect for Low's unusual kindnesses. He hails from those well-to-do men who could lose their wealth without losing any of the love they enjoy; for he, with his integrity and activity, would be able to make another fortune for himself. He inherited his wealth from his father, but the gifts of resignation, humility, industriousness and benevolence come from himself. He considers that a rich man should not be a gilded parasite reared on a golden goblet, but a lively being, a harp played to the human winds, and a useful combatant in the enormous and complicated battles of life. He is already prepared to occupy his high position and work from it for the public good, the free vote,

8. Henry Clay (1777-1852), Senator from Kentucky, known as the "Great Compromiser," Secretary of State (1825-1889).

9. Abraham Lincoln (1809-1865), was elected sixteenth president of the United States on the Republican ticket. He was not an Abolitionist, but, while hating slavery, stood until 1863 solely for opposition to the further extension of slavery in the territories and not for the total abolition of slavery.

10. James Abram Garfield (1831-1881), Union brigadier-general during the Civil War, Republican leader after the war, and was elected president on the Republican ticket in 1880. Garfield was shot by Charles Guiteau on July 2, 1881, and died September 9, 1881.

useful schools, rapid means of communication, and not to do anything
that turns out to be done without the fear of God, of himself, and
of men's censure. . . .

M. DE Z.

La Opinión Nacional, Caracas, November 26, 1981

MARTI'S LETTERS

THE TARIFF BATTLE. — POLITICAL CORRUPTION. — ABUSES OF THE REPUBLICAN PARTY. — REFORMS: ATTEMPTS AND PROMISES. — IRON MAGNATES AND SUGAR MAGNATES. — THE DEMOCRATS' SITUATION. — IDENTICAL IMMORALITY OF ALL THE PARTIES. — FIRST ANNOUNCEMENTS OF THE FORMATION OF A NEW POLITICAL PARTY. — A CARICATURE.

New York, February 21, 1883

To the Editor of *La Nación:*

. . . New York's eyes are now focussed upon Washington. And not because Representative Cox,[1] a young orator, fills his enemies' shields with well-aimed arrows; not because the austere Democrat Randall,[2] a gentleman of note who is generally referred to as a Presidential candidate favored by the country, shouts Shakespeare's "Be a man!" to a Congressman that insults him; not because in the joyous festivities where the ladies of our America are accustomed to bedazzle with the light of beauty, and our diplomatic envoys with the light of the intellect—the Republican court's sumptuous and troubled winter comes to a brilliant close. In Washington the tariff battle is now under way. In Washington the projected trade agreement with Mexico has just been presented to the people.

Politics is a priesthood when impelled by a great national peril or a grand soul. There are creatures who come out of themselves, overflow with love, need to give of themselves, and bring to the world an invisible sword, always held high, which lights the battle-fields with its brilliance as long as they live, and when they fall to the ground covered with all of their armor, it flies like a blue flame to the sun. But politics becomes villainy when it is practised as a mere trade. The United States is offering this spectacle now, for the country is determined to remove the sorcerers from their chairs, and seat priests in their places.

1. Samuel Sullivan Cox (1824-1889), member of the House of Representatives from New York (1869-1873, 1873-1885); proposed tariff and Civil Service reforms. Often referred to as "Sunset Cox."

2. Samuel Jackson Randall (1828-1890), Democratic Congressman from Pennsylvania (1863-1890); Speaker of the House of Representatives (1876-1881).

One word describes the impression the last elections made upon the Republicans who considered themselves masters of the country: dread. In the November elections the nation slapped their cheeks with the evidence of their wrongdoings. And like a salesman in a store surprised in some shortcoming, who fears for the position he is not honoring, and goes about filled with dread and attempting to flatter the owner whom he fears—the Republicans put ashes upon each other's foreheads, and offered penance. They are accused of using in unnecessary and fraudulent projects the huge excess of annual taxes upon the year's expenditures. They are accused of deliberately keeping in effect the war taxes, the high customs duties, and the highly increased taxes levied upon certain national industries, in order to thus fill the State treasury for the benefit of accomplices, powerful voters, and monopolists. They are accused of preventing the great masses in the country from buying at a fair price the necessities of life because they refuse to make a judicious reduction in the excessively high tariffs now placed upon these articles, their sole objetive being that of freeing from foreign competition a small number of industries which, thanks to high tariffs, impose upon the nation their inferior products at a higher price. And the accusation was so imposing that the penance had to seek some shape without delay.

So then the Republicans announced that it was a part of their program in the present Congressional campaign to lower by some seventy-five million dollars the tariffs now paid by the nation. But since the seed is in the fruit, preserving the interests which these measures affect is fundamental to the Republican Party. There is a worm in its marrow. The Party is composed of elements which those reforms would hurt in their very entrails. Rare is the Republican representative who—in addition to his party's general compromises with the large quantity of producers protected by the prohibitive laws and the protectionist tariff—is not tied to some partial compromises with the many producers of his State who are always the powerful voters. Reform was indispensable. Demanding it is to decrease, and perhaps impoverish, the protected industries. Every Republican representative then, was disposed to vote for lowering all tariffs except those affecting his own constituency.

The sugar magnates paid little attention to the harm which the reduction in foreign iron import duties might cause to the iron

34

magnates, provided that there would be no lowering of the duties that burden foreign sugar and thus permit them to obtain a fair profit from selling domestic sugar to the poor. But it made little difference to the iron magnates, provided that iron from abroad was not permitted to enter the country, that domestic sugar might be endangered once foreign sugar had been freed from import duties. The Senate was presented with a bill which, with a cut in sugar duties, would curtail tariffs by some twenty millions of dollars at no great risk to the sugar magnates; yet this curtailment gave a sign of respect and repentance to the nation that proved to be unhappy and angry in the November elections.

But since those industries are the very flesh of the Republican Party, it cannot hurt any of them profoundly without imparing its own strength. One tariff reduction having been brought about, it is inappropriate to bring about another. And if it makes one reduction it cannot make another, because the complaints of its friends and supporters would be greater than those of its complaining enemies.

The dominant elements keeping the Republican Party afloat do not yield one iota in the protectionist doctrines which are in fact the reasons for their support. The politicians would yield—to please the people, and to keep themselves secure in the saddle; but their dealings with the voters bind the politicians more securely than the golden chain bound the Roman gatekeeper to the gate.

The iron magnates announced that they would defeat the plan to lower the duties upon sugar if, in defiance of the popular outcry and in the face of the accusing Republic, the indeterminate protection of every iron industry in the United States was not guaranteed by a tariff increase on foreign iron. And since some Republicans do not dare to favor such a measure, others are destroying the projected reduction. Republicans defeated Republicans.

With their niggardly reforms they wanted to provoke the Democrats to vehement opposition to the projected plans, to make those Democrats appear before the nation as incorrigible disruptors and the real enemies of the Republicans' attempt at improvement. But the sensible Democrats seemed disposed to vote for the plan which the Republicans may have made public solely to have it defeated. And since the latter's conflicting interests are now demolishing the reform plan, the dagger is beginning to be turned against their breasts, and the Republicans are once again shown to be the nation's scoffers and the defenders of personal interest cliques rather than of the great national interests, thus leaving the Democrats with a spotless reputation as apostles and executors of the much desired tariff under whose banner they will doubtless engage in a glorious battle in the coming elections.

Why recount trifles? Everything points to the supreme need: taking public business out of the hands of those who profit from it. After the Democrats come to power, will they perhaps show more independence? Virtue is open to suspicion when it is on the side of interest, and when triumph resides only in the exercise of virtue.

There are protectionist Democrats of no little worth, nor are they few in number. There is a rumour in the factories, docks, and mines, that if foreign products were allowed free entry or low import duties, this country's workers would be left without employment. But since there is room for a large reduction in government expenditures, and today there are excess funds from import tariffs, the Democrats will cut the entire surplus of taxes which certain national industries now pay, and other surplus domestic taxes which today are harshly burdening essential consumer goods, and will free from duties the foreign products not manufactured to any great extent in the United States. This means that the people's outcries will be heard, the concern spreading among the workers will be taken care of, living costs will be greatly reduced, and the protectionist system firmly entrenched for quite some time.

But just as opposition is obligatorily coupled with virtue, in politics—after one's feet are securely placed in lordly dominance—victory is generally coupled with misconduct. And due to the fact that here and everywhere the victorious Democrats usually do not do anything better than the victorious Republicans, the public vote might beautifully and definitively rise in revolt in the not too distant future, and seek a way of rectifying and applying itself in a new and stainless way, which would help its representatives avoid the risk of being left powerless to make laws—for their power is leased to the mighty manufacturers who contribute to electing them—or of putting their hands upon unlawful profit, shady protection, and vice-ridden gain.

Now a periodical of caricatures that vividly describes the people of other lands—and therefore perhaps reflects those of this one so truthfully and courageously that it arouses the attention and has gained some fame—is now depicting—among the dead or badly wounded, or people clothed in rags and tatters or flimsy dented armor, who represent the old parties—an innocent and arrogant youth of frank bearing, open shirt, wide breeches, and stout boots. As if having appeared by some stroke of magic and a pure gust of wind from the bowels of the earth, he gazes sternly at the clear horizon, the fields to till, and the new world, his hand upon a plow. And the periodical calls this youth the "new party."

All evidence shows that suffrage is not running smoothly. There is nothing better than suffrage, but there is still room for improvement.

The man who goes to the Legislature filled with gratitude and favors received, and with tacit or expressed association with the political boss who appointed him, cannot be an honest representative. Such slaves cannot be men charged with defending freedom!

Certain intellectually and financially important men who have congregated in New York to set their eyes upon public affairs, are doing well, then, to nominate respectable and proven candidates who will never leave the bosom of their group. They are doing well to distribute the work of vigilance among diverse commissions which will take charge respectively of examining the various branches of public administration. They are acting wisely in snatching State business away from the cohort of professional political busy bodies—who usually derive from it patronage and benefits for their favorites, as did the viceroys of our lands—and in returning them to the respectable hands of serious and upright men who protect national interests the way the knights of old protected their ladies, and who accept the duty of managing them as a venerable investiture and a sacred trust. The evil triumph only when the good are indifferent.

JOSÉ MARTÍ

La Nación, Buenos Aires, March 31, 1883

POLITICAL AFFILIATION

THE ORIGIN OF THE REPUBLICAN PARTY IN THE UNITED STATES

New York, October 20, 1884

To the Editor of *La Nación:*

No political party had a more glorious birth than the Republican Party of the United States, because none was formed by more unselfish ambitions or nobler hopes.

This country's Constitution was stained by one original vice: it had compromised with the slavery of a race.[1] The Republican Party was actually founded to cleanse it of that stain.[2] It was not composed solely of the best among the living. It can also be said that it was composed of the illustrious dead. The shadows of Washington, Jefferson, Franklin, and Hamilton presided over its sessions, and the great ancestors of North American liberty took part in spirit in the work of recasting, in which the pure gold was going to be separated from the dross.

As one historian of that beautiful movement points out, the seeds of slavery and of liberty fell upon this continent's soil at the same time. In 1620 the *Mayflower* brought the Pilgrims to Plymouth

1. The issue of slavery in the Constitution is reflected in the provision that gave the southern states the right to import slaves for a period of twenty years without fear of unfavorable legislation by the federal Congress; the provision that three-fifths of a slave should be counted in the apportionment of both representatives in the lower house of Congress and direct taxes, and the provision that fugitive slaves escaping from one state to another were to be returned to their owners. The Constitution, however, did not mention the words "slavery" or "slave."

2. The Republican Party was founded in 1854 after passage of the Kansas-Nebraska Act which repealed the Missouri Compromise limiting slavery to a line south of 36° 30'. The Republicans did not call for the abolition of slavery, but did oppose its further expansion into new territories.

and in 1620 a Dutch ship brought twenty African slaves to Virginia.[3] Never has a more extraordinary parallelism been seen. The nucleus of the social discipline which dignified the citizens' obedience because it deprived public authority of all iniquitous force—and together with that, degrading work and vilifying property, placed piracy among the country's basic institutions: the Black slave trade. Thus did the United States begin its life.

The Declaration of Independence had said these memorable words: "We hold these truths to be self-evident, that all men are created equal. . . ."[4] But the Declaration of Independence was the genuine expression of the great spirit that animated the heroes and preachers of liberty—the spirit that fought the Battle of Bunker Hill and triumphed at Yorktown. The political constitution, on the other hand, was only a pact—*a pact with the devil,* as Wendell Phillips was later to call it.[5]

The determination to establish the Union, and the determination, afterward, to maintain it, were superior to the magnanimous hatred with which the infamous institution was regarded in the northern and eastern States.

Those who wished to erase the ominous stain, even at the greatest cost and with their own blood, had to proceed against and fight the wisdom of that patriotism—which put the Union above

3. Actually, the date for the introduction of Negroes into Virginia was 1619. These Blacks, moreover, were not slaves but indentured servants who were freed after serving seven years. Slavery, servitude for life, did not begin in Virginia until 1640.

4. The "memorable words" continue: "that they are endowed by their Creator with inherent and inalienable rights, that among these are life, liberty and the pursuit of happiness." In a section of the original Declaration of Independence, as written by Thomas Jefferson, King George III of England was attacked for violating the "most sacred rights of liberty" by the capturing of "a distant people and carrying them into slavery into another hemisphere." But this clause was deleted as a result of the opposition of southern slaveholders and northern supporters of the slave trade.

5. As a devoted follower of William Lloyd Garrison, Wendell Phillips believed that the Constitution was a pro-slavery document. Garrison argued that in giving "solemn guarantees" to slavery, the Constitution was "a covenant with death, and an agreement with hell."

all ideas and sentiments.[6] In the South they were called criminals and in the North fanatics; in the South the slave owners took them to court and from there to the gallows; in the North the merchants and statesmen considered them to be excitable and dangerous people whom they found it necessary to silence and whom they were disposed to offer as propitiatory victims to southern vengeance. Thus seen, the Union signified naught but material agrandizement: vast cotton fields, great sugar cane and tobacco plantations, gigantic stills. In order to prevent the Union from being this alone, one cold and snowy night—January 6 of 1832—twelve men of good will met in a Boston church and signed the constitution of the anti-slavery party.[7] They were as poor and humble as those of Galilee, and the gospel which their words were going to plant in the cold hearts of their fellow citizens was doubtless the same as the one which their Puritan forebears came to freely read upon this virgin soil of America. In order to raise it above the slave's head as a sign of protection, and above the slave-trader's lash as an anathema of condemnation, they waged the magnificent campaign for whose enthusiastic proclamation Garrison, their chief, was dragged through the streets and heaped with insults.[8] But it was to end with Gettysburg's laurels, Lincoln's Emancipation Proclamation,[9] the defeat and prodigious destruction of the titanic power which had been nourished by the Negroes' blood, and the thirteenth amendment to

6. Martí refers here to Garrison's slogan, "No Union with Slave-holders." Garrison believed that abolitionists should do everything in their power to bring about the dissolution of the Union, and "come out" of the "blood-soaked" relationship between North and South.

7. The reference is to the formation of the New England Anti-Slavery Society, with William Lloyd Garrison as secretary. The society's constitution stressed immediate emancipation of the slaves, improvement of the lot of the free Blacks, and opposition to colonization of free Blacks in Africa.

8. William Lloyd Garrison (1805-1879), founder of the *Liberator,* an anti-slavery journal and leader of the abolitionists who called for immediate emancipation, was dragged through the streets and almost lynched by a pro-slavery mob in Boston on October 21, 1835. To protect him from the mob, Garrison was placed in the city jail.

9. Issued at first by President Abraham Lincoln on September 23, 1862, the Emancipation Proclamation provided that all slaves would be declared free in those states still in rebellion against the United States on January 1, 1863. On that day President Lincoln issued the final Emancipation Proclamation freeing all slaves except those in the border states of Delaware, Kentucky, Maryland, and Missouri, and those parts of the Confederacy already occupied by Union troops. The Proclamation also opened the door to the unlimited use of Blacks, including slaves, in the Union Army.

the North American Constitution[10] which Washington would have wished to sign:[11] a charter of liberty for five million helots, and a charter of rehabilitation and justice for thirty million citizens.

It would certainly be interesting to write the history of that propaganda if the nature of this journalistic work would permit it. It would be an act of piety and justice to leave flowers upon the gravestone lying in the "Way of the Cross" of great human memories—a stone that guards the remains of martyrs and heroes. And so would it be to repeat the sublime words of the orators and poets who gave moving expression to the sobs of the unfortunate and the indignation of the good, and in which in Whittier's Pindaric stanzas,[12] in Bryant's majestic cantos,[13] in that unforgettable novel which shed light upon the inmost recesses of slavery,[14] in those newspaper columns written by the pen of a Greeley,[15] near the pulpits from which the voices of a Beecher or a Channing[16] resounded, in those legislative sessions where an Adams [17] or a

10. The Thirteenth Amendment to the Constitution of the United States was approved by Congress on February 1, 1865 and ratified by the required number of states within the same year. It provided that slavery shall no longer exist within the United States or any place under its jurisdiction.

11. This reference is not clear since George Washington did not call for the abolition of slavery.

12. John Greenleaf Whittier (1807-1892), anti-slavery poet and editor of *The Voices of Freedom* (1846).

13. William Cullen Bryant (1794-1878), poet and editor active in the anti-slavery cause.

14. The reference is to *Uncle Tom's Cabin*, the great anti-slavery novel by Harriet Beecher Stowe (1811-1896).

15. In his editorials in the New York *Tribune*, Horace Greeley opposed slavery and the Mexican war, and supported the Republican Party.

16. William Ellery Channing (1780-1842), leader of Unitarianism, pastor of Federal Street Church, Boston (1803-1842). While not an abolitionist, he spoke out and wrote against slavery.

17. John Quincy Adams (1767-1848), sixth president of the United States, who served in the House of Representatives from Massachusetts (1831-1848), where he played a major role in opposing slavery and its expansion.

Sumner[18] hurled the sidereal splendors of their great words and a reflection of their conscience upon the mercantile debates of obscure congressional sessions—in short, in all that work of powerful fantasy and purest emotion, those words shine with the classic beauty which has never failed the sincere and enthusiastic revelation of human ideas.

The battle had to be waged everywhere: in meetings, in the press, in books, in churches as well as in the Capitol, in the noisy streets as well as in household conversations. Two hostile spirits, two currents of opposing ideas were stirring this immense country and violently shaking its institutions, fighting to dominate them forever. The first words against the Union were extracted from the generous faction by pain and shame. *King Cotton,* for so was slavery sarcastically called, seemed too strong at the time to dream about dethroning it without severing the ties. "Since the Union is infamy, *delenda Cartago!*" cried Wendell Phillips. "I thank heaven that it has been a long time since I've considered myself a United States citizen." The most passionate, in fact, refused to get involved with the political life of the Republic. We cannot do so, they said, without swearing to defend the Constitution, and that oath would be sacrilege. We do not desire a Union with the slave traders. This democracy is not a model but a scandal for the whole world. To purify us from the ignorance which it throws upon us and upon our children, we must sever all connections with the crime; *down with the national authority which protects it, and the national Church which gives it its blessing.*

When the propaganda increased, there was nothing more frequent than the electric shock of opinions, in public as well as private life. The clamor of conflicting passions, and of the inflamed, wounding, and harsh language with which the adversaries appealed to one another, was to be heard in hotel meeting rooms as well as from the benches of Congress. Slavery had its priests just as it was later to have its martyrs; it had its psalms, prayers, and interpreters of

18. Charles Sumner (1811-1874), U. S. Senator from Massachusetts (1851-1874), a bitter foe of slavery and firm advocate of equality for Blacks, Sumner was physically attacked on the floor of the Senate in 1856 by Representative Brooks of South Carolina, and was incapacitated for several years. He was returned to the Senate by his constituents during this period.

the Bible. At first, even the southerners called it a "necessary evil";
later, carried along by the vertigo of the polemic, justification for
the slave trade was raised to a dogma.[19] For the southerner the
attack upon slavery was a threat against his property, a disregard
for his rights, a design of a federal tyranny, and finally an outrage—
it amazes one to say so—an outrage against his religious beliefs!
The man of the South believed in slavery as he believed in God.

The Republican Party was finally formed after some different
and fragmentary organizations, which were like its rehearsals. Calm
men of serene spirit, political tact, and good sense that bordered on
genius, following the line of fire of their tempestuous precursors,
came to embody in reality and implant in the soil the ideas of
dreamers and prophets. So it must be for justice and beauty to
triumph in the world. An imperishable tribute and a most grateful
memory for those who, in society or in art, are breaking the molds
in which ideas are able to live when feverish hands stirred by
inspiration and enthusiasm are placed upon them. But let us bless the
law of Nature which has given birth beside them—perhaps below
them—to men capable of confining the thundering torrent to a river
bed, although not with all the volume of its waters, so that the
crowds may drink from it. Garrison and Wendell Phillips had wished
to dissolve the Union; Abraham Lincoln came to consolidate it.[20]

The Republican Party did not unfurl the banner of abolition.[21] The
eminent and most noble task of presenting the redemptive idea to
the nation's conscience had fallen to others; apostles and poets had

19. The "necessary evil" doctrine was replaced by the "positive good"
theory, which proclaimed that slave labor was essential for the development of the nation; that the Negro was destined to be kept in
subordinate position; that slaves were better fed, better clothed,
and happier than either the free Blacks or white workers in the North
and England.

20. At first the Garrisonians, with Wendell Phillips as a leading spokes-
man, favored letting the southern states secede and depart from the
Union. But after the firing on Fort Sumter, they supported Lincoln's
position of maintaining the integrity of the Union by force if necessary.

21. The Republican platform in 1860 declared that "the normal condition of
all the territory of the United States is that of freedom. . . and we
deny the authority of Congress, of a territorial legislature, or of any
individuals, to give legal existence to slavery in any territory of the
United States." But it also assured the South that each state had
the "right to order and control its own domestic institutions according
to its own judgement exclusively."

proclaimed it: "Let us no longer be satisfied" said Whittier with magnificent poetry; "let us not be resigned to speaking the truth softly and in cowardly whispers; let us speak in resounding voices; like the sounds of a bugle." A necessary and sublime indiscretion. But men who were going to struggle at the ballot boxes, who would prefer slow victory to heroic defeat, who had the vocation and faculties of political combat, had to choose another terrain and other weapons for the definite duel. In the state of public opinion, given the resources and the respective situations of the factions dividing the country, abolition as a political program was an absurd undertaking. The Republican Party confined itself to rejecting the recent agreements which the North, intimidated by the energy of the South, had contracted with it.[22] These agreements enlarged to immense proportions the breach which the Constitution had opened. One cannot think but that the free states were moving backward before the irresistible invasion of slavery. Every new Congress, because of southern energy and the mercantile fears of the North, opened new bazaars to the iniquitous slave trade, and sullied a new piece of territory with the poisonous shadow of servitude. The agreements permitted that which had always been denied by the North, a spread of the gangrene. Within a short time, had the Republican Party not hindered that spread, the words spoken by Daniel Webster referring to Ohio no longer could have been repeated: "The 1787 law stamped upon the soil itself, when it was still covered by forest, the impossibility of its being trodden by slaves."[23]

In 1860 Abraham Lincoln, the calmest and most serene enemy of slavery—a man among those who are called providential because they respond to all the demands of the ministry that is their lot—rose to power by two million votes, and carried with him to the famous White House the banner of the Republican Party.[24] It is unnecessary to recall southern anger, the broken treaty, Buchanan's

22. The reference is to the Compromise of 1850 and the Kansas-Nebraska Act of 1854, both of which extended slavery.

23. The ordinance of 1787, passed by Congress, prevented the extension of slavery into the states to be formed from these territories. Ohio was one of these states.

24. Lincoln was elected President as the Republican Party candidate in the election of 1860. He did not win a plurality of the popular vote but a majority of the electoral college vote.

miserable conduct,[25] Europe's jubilation because of the mutilation of the colossus, and the numerous and extraordinary vicissitudes of the war. On January first of 1863, using a power which the most authorized interpretation of constitutional law acknowledged for him, the President of the United States, as a punishment for the rebels and because of the supreme dictate of the war, proclaimed the slaves in the South free.[26] Painting, poetry, and eloquence have preserved for us the picture of that Cabinet meeting in which Lincoln rose to his feet and read the proclamation to his ministers; he wrote it himself in that style, which history must not alter, that impresses ideas upon the mind at once. "I know how impatient you are," he added. "I wanted this to be done before; but I was waiting for the right moment." And later, in such a low voice that it could barely be heard: "When Lee was thrown out of Maryland, I promised my God that the slaves would be emancipated." It is a known fact that the abolitionists did not consider their work concluded; renowned are the laws and the institutions of piety and teaching with which they tried to raise the downtrodden race to the highest level possible. A few years after the war, an eyewitness related that an aged Negro woman was kneeling in the street beside a Republican school in the South. When asked what she was doing there, she replied: "It is too late for me to enter, but I'm praying for the founders of this school where my grandchildren can go to learn."

Therefore, in the early years of its existence, the Republican Party, wise in counsel, titanic in war, great and strong in word and deed—accomplished one of humanity's heroic undertakings, and made a heaven in history. Upon the country's flag, held aloft by that party, there were no longer any clouds above those incomparable stars, and while beneath its broad folds, the only race exiled

25. The reference is to the secession of the southern states following the election of Abraham Lincoln and the refusal of President James Buchanan to do anything to stop the secession movement. Buchanan's position was that secession was illegal but that he had not power to prevent it.

26. The reference is to the Emancipation Proclamation issued by President Lincoln on January 1, 1863. The Proclamation was issued as a military act by Lincoln as Commander in Chief of the Army. It did not, however, free all the slaves in the South, only those in southern states and parts of southern states which were still in rebellion against the government of the United States. The Thirteenth Amendment to the Constitution, adopted in 1865, ended slavery in the United States.

from civilization was coming forth to a life of justice, there could now be written upon the first page of the Constitution, as if upon enduring granite, the beautiful motto of an eloquent North American orator: "Union and liberty, one and inseparable, now and forever."

JOSÉ MARTÍ

La Nación, Buenos Aires, November 6, 1884

HISTORY OF THE FALL OF THE REPUBLICAN PARTY IN THE UNITED STATES, AND THE RISE TO POWER OF THE DEMOCRATIC PARTY. — ANTECEDENTS, TRANSFORMATIONS AND PRESENT SIGNIFICANCE OF THE PARTIES. — SUMMARY, WITH THE MATTER, OF ALL THE DETAILS AND CONSIDERATIONS WHICH CAN EXPLAIN IN A DEFINITIVE WAY, AS A KEY TO ITS FUTURE MOVEMENTS, NORTH AMERICAN POLITICS.

New York, March 15, 1885

To the Editor of *La Nación:*

I would carve statues in porphyry of the marvellous men who forged the Constitution of the United States of America. I would carve them in a porphyry group, signing their enormous work. I would stretch a sacred road of unpolished marble blocks all the way to a white marble temple to shelter those statues; and every specified number of years I would establish one week of national pilgrimage, in Autumn, the season of ripeness and beauty, so that with the people's reverent heads swathed in clouds of fragrant smoke from the dry leaves, men, women, and children might go to kiss the patriarch's stone hands. Size fails to dazzle me. Wealth fails to dazzle me. I am not dazzled by the material prosperity of a free nation—stronger than its feeble neighbors, isolated from dangerous rivals, favored by the proximity of fertile lands needing to buy its products—to which flows, in the love of liberty and the facility for work, those who are more energetic and enterprising in overpopulated Europe, and the purest and most enthusiastic elements of the humanitarian parties of nations which have not yet broken the shell of feudalism.

Men do not dazzle me, neither do novelties, nor brilliant deeds of daring, nor colossal cohorts. I know that by bringing together so many angry hungry people from different countries—people who fail to embrace one another in love for this country in which they were not born, and whose spirit does not flow in their veins, and who do not derive any other kind of love and concern but for themselves out of fear of life, accumulated in them because of their own and inherited suffering; I know that by bringing together so many egotistic and fearful people, it has followed that the Republic may

53

be largely populated by selfish or indifferent citizens who vote for their own interests, and fail to vote unless they see these interests threatened, and therefore the national government has been slipping out of the citizens' hands, and remaining in the great cliques that traffic with it. I know that the same causes that give rise to prosperity, give rise to indifference. I know that when nations drop the reins, someone picks them up and uses them to whip and oppress, and sits at their head. I know that when men disregard the exercise of their rights in the anxieties, endeavours and perils of luxury, then terrible dangers, lax passions, and disordered justice come about. And trailing them as if to restrain them—like wolves in mastiffs' clothing—comes political centralization, on the pretext of curbing the restless, as does religious centralization, on the pretext of regulating it; and the children accept as salvation both authorities, which their parents abhorred like an insult.

I know that a nation which fails to cultivate the arts of the spirit, coupled with those of commerce, becomes fat as a bull, and will overflow through its own temples, like a spilling of decomposed entrails, when its resources are exhausted. I know that this enormous nation needs honesty and sentiment. But when we see this majesty of the vote, this new nobility of which every living man—tramp or tycoon—forms a part, and this monarch made entirely of heads who cannot wish to hurt himself because he is as big as his whole domain, which is his very self; when we are present at ten million men's unanimous acts of will—we feel as if we were riding a horse made of light, our winged heels hard against its flanks, as if we were leaving an old world of ruins behind us, and as if the doors of a decent world were opening for us to pass through and find enjoyment. Upon the threshold, a woman with an uncovered vessel beside her is washing the torn and mud-spattered brows of the arriving men.

I would carve porphyry statues beneath a marble temple of those who stood up in this new world and with their calm hands affixed a sun of decency on high; of those who sat down to make silken reins for men, and who did make them and did give them to them; of those who perfected man. And I would build a broad white marble road along which to go to worship them.

One cannot see marvels clearly when one is within them. Only at a distance do colossal figures and colossal deeds acquire their natural proportions and appear in their beautiful totality. What does the little worm that crawls in the entrails of majestic beauty know about the human body? It enters by a duct, lodges in a cell, and falls, like a locust upon planted fields, upon the whole tissue. What does that worm—a tiny Lucifer busily transforming the vineyard—know about the pleasant contours of the body which it consumes, about the loving commands—swift and brilliant as starlight—that go from one body to another, about the veil of light in which a lover envelops his beloved, like morning sun the earth? And what does it know about the bower of roses in whose shade they embrace and fall asleep?

A United States Presidential campaign is rough and nauseating. The contest has been in progress since May, before each party selected its candidates. The professional politicians, determined to conduct events so that they can best benefit from them, are not seeking as a Presidential candidate that illustrious man whose virtue merits reward or whose talents can benefit the country; on the contrary, they will seek a man whose craftiness or wealth or special conditions may, even if he is sullied, assure more votes for the party and more influence in the administration for those who contribute to nominating him and seeing to it that he emerge victorious.

Once the candidates are nominated in the Conventions, the mire rises to the saddle pommels. The periodicals' white beards forget the decorum of old age. Pails of mud are dumped upon heads. Lies and exaggerations are knowingly spread. Bellies and backs are slashed. All manner of infamy is considered legitimate. All kinds of blows are good as long as they stun the enemy. Whoever invents an effective villainous act, struts about like a peacock. Even prominent men believe themselves excused from the more trivial duties of honor. Our Latin nobility cannot conceive of such excesses. Behind every phrase one can still see the butts of those pistols with which years ago, and even today from time to time, one argued in the newspapers here at election time. It is a brutal habit which time will heal. In vain does one anxiously read periodicals with quite opposite opinions these months. An observer in good faith fails to know how to analyze a battle in which everyone believes it valid to fight with bad faith. One newspaper flatly denies what another flatly affirms. Each of them purposely curtails all that honors the opposing candidate. In those days they disregard the pleasure of honoring.

The elections are upon us, and the passerby sees only the voting booths in which one votes at one's leisure, the saloons where one goes to waste money and time, and the crowds who pour into the streets to learn the latest news being given out by telegraph to the newspaper bulletins. He sees the vote confused, whisked away, bought, and falsified. He sees naturalized foreigners vote for their special interests to the detriment of the land which is giving them a portion of its wealth and government. He can sense the danger in the country of giving authority to those who were not born in it and do not love it, although he recognizes the justice of giving the vote to each according to the weight each carries. Displeased and alarmed, the country lives from May to November witnessing base acts. But over and above those acts, and even with all of them before our eyes, some respect remains in our minds which have been shaken with astonishment—a respect comparable only to that of a person who has seen a world reeling upon its hinges, leaning toward an abyss, being about to fall, and suddenly regaining its balance. Ten million men acting in unison are a touching sight. He who has seen them, in this time of toil, feels a more solid earth under his feet, and images a crown on his head. This is the inevitable and epic event. Amid this confused and obscure campaign, it shines like a large bronze rose aflame in a gray sky.

No Presidential campaign has been so entangled, transcendental, and significant as the one that gave Grover Cleveland his triumph:[1] Perhaps at a distance the Democratic Party's victory is seen as no more than an obvious event, and one assumes—erroneously—that it implies a decisive change in the country's opinions and trends. From nearby one observes the slightly less than inevitable danger of leaving the country's politics, which in free nations is merely a

1. Grover Cleveland (1837-1908) was elected president of the United States in 1884 on the Democratic ticket. He was the first Democrat to be elected president since the end of the Civil War. The last Democratic President, James Buchanan, was elected in 1856.

way of conducting their interests honorably, in the hands of a class of idle employees who do not possess them. From close at hand one observes how difficult it is to regain the exercise of political power after it has been neglected by upright people. From nearby one sees that the change has not been basic or durable, but occasional and like a test; and one sees what a handful of honest people can do with a shake of the shoulders. Nothing more, nothing more than this—a handful of honest men have given Cleveland his victory. Out of ten million votes, a thousand less would have conferred the Presidency upon a defiled and dismal man, a brilliant sophist—Blaine.[2]

Until the last instant of the race, Blaine and Cleveland were running neck and neck; for many days after the election one did not know whether the White House would display the pine cone, symbol of the Republicans, or the Democratic rooster. Garfield, the Republican, and Hancock,[3] the Democrat, contended four years ago for the Presidency. It is true that this time there were 468,000 more votes for Cleveland than there were then for Hancock, but there were also 393,000 more people voting for Blaine than for that discreet, suffering, good Garfield. Both candidates' victory depended upon one lone State out of the Republic's 36: New York.

The man to win that State would win the Presidency, and Cleveland won the State by a mere thousand votes,[4] although he is its governor. No wonder the indomitable and arrogant Blaine does not admit to being defeated by his adversary but by chance; with subtle knowledge of his nation's hates and fears he is inciting them all, spinning them into a body of doctrine in an admirably skillful

2. James Gillespie Blaine (1830-1893), leader of the Republican Party in Maine, U. S. Senator (1876-1881), unsuccessful candidate for president on the Republican ticket in 1884, and U. S. Secretary of State (1889-1892). Blaine was hated by Martí as representing the worst evils in the United States.

3. Winfield Scott Hancock (1825-1886), Union general who served brilliantly at Gettysburg. After the war he became a leading Democratic politician and was the unsuccessful candidate for president on the Democratic ticket in 1880.

4. On October 29, 1884 the New York minister, Reverend S. D. Burchard, attacked the Democratic Party as the party of "rum, Romanism and rebellion," an action which, it was believed, caused enough votes to be switched from Blaine to Cleveland to enable the latter to carry New York by only 1,149 votes and win the presidency.

speech, and making of them a battle placard with which he proposes
to lead his army to regain the lost power four years from now.

He knows that the North still mistrusts the South, and that the
Democratic administration must be kindly disposed toward it because the great bulk of its adherents are there, and because of
obedience to its spirit and platform; and Blaine, skilled in manipulating men through their passions, and certain that this will in fact
occur, announces and exploits this in advance. Let us then
thoroughly analyze Cleveland's election, for it is most educational.
And if one asks who he is beforehand, we shall say that he is a
man of the people, and although young, one of those old-time
Americans with iron hands and eagle eyes who do not put their
boots on the table, but still wear them. He has the scorn, penetra-
tion, candor, audacity, firmness, and native qualities of the nation
where he was born. His ancestors are the merchant and the ex-
ploiter; the Puritan and the one who tossed the bundles of tea
overboard. His sights are set ahead like someone determined to
make it.

He has the powerful innocence of primary men who stem directly from Nature, and owe less to men than to the influence of
their own originality and their ability to tame them, skillfully blend-
ing the astute submission that flatters them, with the unrestrained
scorn that attracts and retains them; because men and things, evad-
ing whoever solicits them, become attached, by some vile and instinctive sense of slavery, to anyone who wishes to be rid of them.
Great men have to know how to flirt. By serving powerful interests
or preoccupations, it is easy to rise to great positions and be masks
or mouthpieces, as it were, of the forces that elevate men. But when
one realizes how forsaken and alone is honesty, how can one fail
to admire the person who reaches success not because of his
complicity in men's shortcomings, but only when he is opposed to
them. Who stands behind nations, as behind men when despite
those very men, and with a determined and imposing voice, he
confidentially advises what they must do in times of peril, and inspires in them a temporary burst of virtue, which puts them upon
the road to salvation, and sustains them and lifts them up when they
are at the brink of failure? No angel visits Cleveland; the sublime
does not exhaust him and keep his mind in agony; his spirit has

58

the solidity and simplicity of his lunches: bread and butter, a thick slice of meat, a large quantity of tea. He is so simple at times that he seems childish; but in thinking about him, even if only for the man's adjustment to his situation, the name of Lincoln—what praise!—comes to the lips, for Lincoln is the kind of a man who soothes and enlightens when he appears. What are nations waiting for, that they fail to build great temples to men's redeemers, that they fail to place their statues in niches, and write new books about the lives of saints, and assemble on holidays to comment upon their heroes' virtues? Do they clamor for a Church, a Church to replace the one that is vanishing? Well, here is that new Church!

There are two kinds of triumph: one is apparent, brilliant, and temporal; the other is essential, invisible, and enduring. Virtue, always defeated in appearance, triumphs permanently in this second manner. Whoever carries virtue on his shoulders, it is true, has to clutch his heart tightly with both hands, to prevent its being destroyed because of sheer hurt, for men leave the virtuous man's heart so shattered that if he does not sew it together and mend it with his will, it will leap out of him broken into pieces smaller than raindrops. Only in moments of supreme agony, to which dispensing with virtue unavoidably leads nations, do men come to it with great homage and praise, always ready, in times of tribulation, to save those who forget it; and no sooner does virtue take them out of their straits, than they accuse it of being prudish, annoying, inopportune and excessive, and begin to gnaw away at its feet and demolish it.

Men like to be led by those who abound in their own shortcomings. See how they cling more fervently to vicious and brilliant personalities than to pure and modest ones. Only in times of crisis, the instinctive knowledge of great peril and of their inability to rid themselves of it make them accept great and honest men. Integrity irritates them, because they are generally lacking in it. They regard the failings of their rulers as a sanction for their own. By playing a trick on their consciences, they believe that by exonerating those men, they themselves are exonerated. Since his sins do not prevent the statesman from arriving at his high post, sinning, which the world condemns and rewards, is not so wrong. All sinners are secretly sympathetic to sinners. There is nothing like falling into error to learn how to excuse it. Nor is there any greater insolence than that of virtue which, with its stern face, modest clothing, and white hands, makes the people's villainous actions and criminal skills stand out by force of contrast, for when virtue is far away, those actions do not seem so ugly; because everyone has them to the same degree, they are not conspicuous in any one person. So it is that as soon as virtue appears, there are no more stones on the road, because everyone is using them to attack that virtue. Righteousness is a bad road, especially for power. Men follow others only if they are of use to them, and unless constrained to do otherwise, lend their assistance only in exchange for what they receive. The authority which resides in them—because they are citizens of a nation with an electoral government, or because they are persons of influence—they evade or curtail in great measure. Every man is the seed of a despot; as soon as an atom of power falls into his hands, he thinks that Jupiter's eagle is at his side, and that all the worlds are his. That is why in those nations where authority dwells—if not in every citizen then in every overseer of citizens, of which there are countless members—he who aspires to gain people's wills has to diminish his own to such an extent that one fails to know how he can endure the shame occasioned by that conquest of power with greatness of soul. An honest heart turns against those who humiliate in lending their support, at the same time as against those who humiliate themselves because they expect it.

But he who, when needing the influence of a political boss, before procuring him, inquires what his passion is, to flatter it; or what his vanity is, to caress it or his price, to pay it, or the post he covets to promise it to him, he who, fonder of himself than of his people or the human race, weakens in the defense of what he maintains; or abandons it, or defends it more vigorously, according to the wishes of the men he needs in order to obtain command; he who—knowing that reason, convinced of its own sense of justice is overconfident and scornful, and knowing how impressionable and active concern is, responds with all the venom, hatred, and spite that he finds at hand to his opponent's arguments; he who fails to see in his intellectual capabilities a mission of self-sacrificing guardianship of the lesser capabilities, only an effective instrument to disturb them and direct them to his own advantage; he who uses for himself that which he did not receive from himself, and does not contribute to humanity, but corrupts and confounds it; he who does not regard men as brothers in misfortune to comfort and improve, even in spite of themselves, but rather as a socle for his feet, or as a battle of pride and skill, or as the satisfaction of outdoing his competitors in stratagems and wealth; he who views life as nothing but a market place, and men as nothing but pigs to feed, stupid people to mock and, at best, wild animals to shoot down; he who does not have the humanitarian and expansive aspects of genius but only its Catilinarian, Caesarian, and martial traits; he who, as supreme flattery to men, falls into their shortcomings and boasts about them—that man will always have his house filled with clients, and will engage in combat followed by a large number of partisans. That man is Blaine.

Since some persons are busy amassing riches; since many in the battle for their daily bread, are deprived of the well-being which might have moved them to zealous consideration of the good government that should preserve that well-being; and since all of them are abandoned by the solidity that brings to the spirit this precipitate, sumptuary, and avaricious life—politics, although never deserted by prominent and circumspect servants, here was gradually left in the hands of ambitious politicians, employees who help them obtain their posts or remain in them, capitalists who in exchange for laws that are favorable to their undertakings support the party that offers those laws, foreigners who vote according to their interests and passions, and loyal followers who, because they are fond of past glories or old ideas, remember only the national issues, with misunderstood consistence, on days when the elections offer them an opportunity to exercise their authority and confirm their faith.

Great souls, in themselves modest and shy, consent to emerge from themselves only when humanity or their country is in grave danger, and they confront this with astounding daring and Cyclopean courage, later—the battle won and victory assured—to return to the happy corner where one enjoys self-esteem and the affection of a few good people. For these souls there is hardly a greater martyrdom than that of being necessarily confused, in the hour of battle, with the profiteers, businessmen, and fanatics who, like leprosy to healthy skin, become attached to great ideas and at times

are the most visible part of them. The emergence of honest people
was magnificent when the South, exaggerating its power and rights,
was finally determined to move its slave States' wealth away from
the North; and in the light of John Brown's[5] gallows, that inexhaust-
ible army of the North appeared, some with words, some with a
courageous heart, and some giving their entire fortune.

The skies have stars and so does the earth; John Brown's gallows
shines like a star. Jesus died upon the cross, and this man upon
the gallows. After death, men flow into universal existence,
bodiless and with no consciousness of memory; they rise in whirl-
winds, move toward the sun, drift happily; but if after death men
could come together, which they cannot, Jesus and John Brown
would go hand in hand.

Human nature is such that, if the life of an apostle does not
meet with universal recognition, people are ashamed to have it
known that they admire him, and it is considered poor taste even
to praise him. The next group of stars to be discovered might well
be named after John Brown!

Then the most distinguished people from the North responded
to the peril; and the best of all was that long-legged, penny-pinched,
thin-lipped man with the profound glance and sad eyes; the man
who did not hail from merchants, shepherds, or patricians, but from
Nature and bitterness; that poorly dressed man of gracious soul:
good Abe Lincoln. Those men of the North, in an extraordinary
outburst, not only created a party when they organized the Republican
one, they recreated the nation.

They were the new crusaders, and Wendell Phillips was their
Peter the Hermit. They went into every city, assaulted every

5. Leading a group of nineteen men that included five Negroes and his
   own sons, John Brown (1800-1859) attacked the federal arsenal at
   Harper's Ferry, Virginia, October 16, 1859, with the aim of fomenting
   a slave rebellion and eventually establishing a Negro republic in the
   mountains of Virginia. Brown and his men captured the arsenal, but
   the next day a company of U. S. Marines under Colonel Robert E. Lee
   assaulted the group, killed ten, and took Brown prisoner. After a
   hurried trial, the wounded John Brown was sentenced to be tried for
   treason. Brown's bravery and dignity during the trial and on the
   scaffold moved millions of people to regard him as a hero. Among the
   Negro people he was regarded as a saint.

rostrum, spoke from church pulpits, from barrels in the squares, from horseback upon the roads. Not a village without a press; not a day without a speech; not a sojourn without its missionary. They covered their entire country, and then left it to stir others. Thus was the Republican Party established; like a parapet of human freedom.

But as soon as the North was victorious, and the party formed to defend the Union remained in power as its symbol, and the Democratic Party that caused the disturbance, and which was dominant in the rebel States was out of power the Republic dazzled as it was by victory and the colossal prosperity stemming from it scarcely paid any attention to the details of national affairs whose management is considered a timely reward for those who had saved it. The North devoted itself fervently to the amassing of wealth. Their duty fulfilled, the generous men who had consented to abandon their humility only in the face of a great peril, were returning to their homes and tasks.

The Republican Party remained in the hands of those who —whether because of fondness for their victories, or hatred of their enemies, or fear that they might revive, or for their own benefit—had a more direct interest in keeping it organized and powerful. And since victory corrupts, decomposition commenced immediately thereafter. The manifesto of human liberty turned into a house of usury.

What distribution of the best positions to inept men, like sinecures! What distribution of surplus revenue in confused expenses! What contracting, at scandalous cost, for non-existent mail trains and ships that capsized in the first rough seas! What giving of employment—to the detriment of the more worthy and honest—to those who were protected by powerful men and women or had worked in a servile capacity in the shady deals of the elections! What an accumulation, with secret promises and immoral deals, of enormous sums to defeat the Democrats in the Presidential campaigns! What promises to employees of permanent positions, provided that they aid the electoral fund with their contributions, thereby keeping the party in government! What handing over of the nation's lands and even its rights, law by law, to capitalists and powerful associations,[6] in previously stipulated payments of enormous subsidies which, to assure the party's remaining in power, it received from monopolies and speculators in hard times! What cynical response to the accusations of their opponents, and to the best men of their own party—whom the spectacle of such bold corruption had forced to break their silence—accusing them of being masked friends of the rebellion! Who leaves liberty without vigilance? Who fails to know that for every dove that is born, there are worms born as big as three doves? In the elections, what vote-buying, or changing them in the ballot boxes, or reducing their number on the lists, when the need arises! In the lesser State assemblies which elect delegates to the Convention where the party's Presidential candidate is nominated, what exclusion, accusing them of treason, of those who refused to vote in the interests of the professional politicians!

In the Conventions themselves, at the time of nominating the candidate, what scorn for the illustrious men of tried and true reputation by those of recognized faults who, thanks to those very faults, might with less scruples secure more votes in the election and more employment and profit in power! And how the Convention's delegates sell themselves to this or that petitioner for the candidacy either for money or the promise of a good position, in case of victory!

The once glorious Conventions, in which those delegated by the party in each State gather every four years to elect their candidate for the nation's primary position, have become an open market, where honor is bought and sold in back rooms. An entire delegation was bought with a few thousand dollars, just as this kind of a delegate, in order to be one, had always bought the nomination in this evil way in the State assembly, by virtue of which he could then sell his vote in the National Convention. And there was never a lack of money for these purchases of wavering delegations, because there were so many enormous corporations and so many bold promoters interested in the victory of the candidate who has promised

6. The reference is to the assistance to private railroads by federal and state governments in the form of land grants, loans, right of way, tax exemption. Land grants were the most substantial form of public aid to railroads.

to be at their beck and call in recompense for these advances. So the respected people withdrew from the last Convention as from a profaned temple.

The Democratic Party's return to power was proclaimed a national calamity and a triumph of the South, by which the adherence of the northern States was secured.

The best men kept themselves apart from public affairs because they disliked publicity, or did not wish to appear in public arm in arm with profiteers, and those who had no special interest remained apart because of indifference. So, sure of triumph and impunity, and in agreement with the written and spoken declarations of the most important Republicans, one could say that there was no public abuse, violation, fraud, bribery, plundering or theft that the Republican Party had not inspired or encouraged.

In the elections, Democratic ballots were substituted for Republican ones, or the latter were increased at will, or the count was falsified. In the States, money set aside for public affairs disappeared into private purses. In Washington, the Cabinet bought the support of congressmen in both Houses with positions and pensions for the people whom it recommended. A certain number of posts were reserved for every senator and representative to distribute among their favorites, and "in many cases," says the Honorable Mr. Veagh, a member who served in Garfield's Cabinet, "the men for whom this privilege is reserved, and the women appointed by virtue of it (for it is a well-known fact that in the United States many employees are women) live far from the shelter and bonds of their homes."

In the office of the Secretary of War, all was broken cash boxes, "double accounts," and forage for an imaginary cavalry. One could not enter the Secretary of the Interior's office without stumbling against a clique of pension agents, Indian Funds agents, Land Dis-

tribution agents whose revenue, once granted to the clique, would
go largely in payment to those who had assisted in securing the
concession. In the Postal clique, new contracts were given to the
contractor, who had been indicted for receiving real subsidies for
false services. In the treasury clique, a thief of treasury bills
became so powerful that when one of the indignant Cabinet members
wanted to lay hands on him, there was another Cabinet member, if
not more than one, who interceded for the robber and saved him.
In the Foreign Affairs clique, was there not an entire mission con-
trived, face to face with a war, in hopes of obtaining the recognition of some immoral private claim—a pretext, if not for base
profit or for an undeserved and abusive protectorate, then for
dandyism and diplomatic foolishness, unworthy of an honored and
serious nation?

With such great abuses occurring, they were finally arousing
the indignation and energy of the party's soundest and less visible
members; first in the private councils, later, still silently, in the
election battles, and in the end openly at the Convention that nominated Blaine; and in the campaign in which he was defeated, those
sound members made public their determination to purify the dishonored party or leave it. They were called Pharisees, coxcombs,
and traitors. On the occasion of the candidate's nomination, and
the electoral fight that followed, the tendencies which had been
secretly dividing the Republican Party were accentuated and defined;
and even before—because some blood must precede every fruitful
work in the ferocious human contest—they had come to cause
the death of Garfield, by inciting a disordered mind.[7] There were
two groups. One group impudently maintained that, above any other
consideration, there were party interests and its members' benefits;
that the Union was the natural property of those who had rescued
it; that to the victor belong the spoils; that the positions, concessions, and dignities must go toward paying for the services loaned
to maintain in power the party that grants them; that it is not
censurable but lawful to collect from public employees, paid with
funds advanced by the entire nation, sums destined to keep in the
government one of the parties that fight for it. And in exchange for

7. Garfield was shot by Charles J. Guiteau, a disgruntled office seeker,
and died September 9, 1881. Guiteau was tried, found guilty, and
executed. Martí wrote extensively about the events following the
shooting of President Garfield, and covered Guiteau's trial in detail.

this assistance it is obligated to keep the contributors in its employment, since they are now its accomplices, and to protect or conceal their abuses. The other group—sons in spirit of the Republic's monumental founders—accused that program of being abominable. And even if well disposed to keeping the Republican organization alive as a still necessary symbol of the Union—which was yesterday threatened, as a moderating and principally domestic party, as a wise repressor of the excessive and foreign factional influence that seems to be noted in the Democratic Party which is composed largely of southern voters and many from Ireland and Germany—they nonetheless preferred the party's temporary if not definitive dissociation, or perhaps a fusion of its better faction with the more exalted and doctrinal faction of the Democrats, rather than contribute with their complicity in keeping the national government in the hands of an aggressive crowd of stubborn profiteers.

What was the nucleus of this colossal power, the key to this enormous machine, the barrier placed against the best efforts of the Party's sincere people, the obstacle to all attempts at its moralization and reform—if not the faculty of distributing positions and public properties among its assistants? What more perspicacious and zealous agents can a party have than those who owe it their livelihood, and who without that party—since they are accustomed to easy well-being and idleness—are reduced to inconsideration and misery? They were, then, the party's servants and propagandists, not its sincere followers who give their services without pay and therefore enjoy making their influence felt, but those who depend upon it for their livelihood, and to whom lofty examples and a desire to support themselves in placid wealth encouraged to achieve some influence with which to serve their party at election time, and to serve the complicities and illicit exemptions which permit the exercise of a benevolently guarded authority.

Most of the unaware majority took a long time to reflect upon this corruption. The common people, even the enlightened ones, considered it dangerous to return the government to the Democrats, in whose councils the spirit of the South was still thought to be predominant. And since an almost marvellous prosperity had occurred following the war under the Republicans who had won it, patriotism and interest joined hands to maintain confidence in the victorious party. Despite its blunders and abuses, this party was given credit for the abundant harvests, the vast sums that entered the country in return for them, and the application of this surplus wealth to the creation of industries which seemed prosperous—due to the fact that the domestic market was still sufficiently large to consume its manufactured articles—because the surplus of exports over imports permitted paying, without heavy losses, the immoderate prices at which competitive American products were sold because of the high tariffs on European imports.

After the enormous war came enormous confidence and the blinding wealth that carries one away and attracts everything to itself in the eagerness to enjoy it and the fear of losing it. So while the dazzled country was given over in true frenzy to its extraordinary undertakings, the birds of prey took advantage of this to build their nests in the national tree until it was finally apparent and undeniable that the lengthy stay in power of men who in its shadow had lost the habit, and perhaps the capacity, of a more honorable manner of living; the security of constant victory; the practice of spending national funds upon party expenses; the intimacy with businessmen who charge dearly for services rendered— all these factors had made the ruling party insolent and shameless at the same time that its motives were perverted. For with practice, when not by law, the party in power was curtailing the country's means of shaking it off and replacing it with the opposing one. For this reason, as soon as the country felt the yoke upon its neck, it demolished the party with a single blow.

Emboldened by its predominance, the Republican Party obviously paid no attention to calming the anxiety which the surplus of unsalable products, and too much unemployment, was starting to cause, and quite justifiably so. It was obvious that to be able to continue distributing among their favorites the surplus unnecessarily collected by import duties, the Republicans refused to lower them on the pretext of protecting national industries—which are dying from this protection. For the party was actually merely raising the cost of living for a population already afflicted by unemployment. And this was inescapably caused by the surplus production of articles which, due to their abundance and high prices, cannot find buyers in this alarmed and amply supplied nation, nor could those articles compete

68

with less expensive and better ones made abroad. It was evident that with such shameless support by venal legislators, the laws tended to concentrate the wealth, as well as the power, with increasing loss of the States' and citizens' independence, and with curtailment of the possibilities of enterprise, which the monopolies are absorbing, and without whose hope the useful workers are becoming discontent and rebellious. It was evident that with the bond between employees and government, and the Republic's resources being used for the private expenditures of one of its political parties, it was going to become impossible, in the long run, to wrest authority from a party whose abuses and arrogance were provoking condemnation of its leading men, and whose economic errors, continued in support of notorious interests, have brought the country—by deceitfully favoring the maintenance of artificial industries—to a latent and anguished crisis which is paralyzing and alarming everyone and everything. The nation will be able to recover from this only by means of its agricultural production, aided by a reduction in living costs because of a more rational and tolerable tariff, and by reducing industrial production to articles which the United States can manufacture without a fictitious tariff, with a real possibility of being victorious in competing with its foreign rivals. All available land must be cultivated—and never with only a single crop. Regarding industries, none but natural and direct ones.

As soon as the nation began to suffer from a depressed commerce, it investigated the causes, and found them to be in large part due to a partial and casual management of national affairs. The country was a banquet, and the fat successful Republicans were permanently seated at the table. Political wounds, like bodily wounds, heal themselves as long as one is careful not to poison or reopen them. Just as the flesh grows and draws the open edges together with new tissue, so the cure, as its natural benefit, springs from excessive wrongs. The laws of politics are identical to the laws of Nature. The moral world is equal to the material world. The laws that govern the course of a star through space are the laws that govern the development of an idea through the mind. All things are identical. When, because of an appetite for wealth outside of the government and immorality within it, the nation seemed rotten to the core and susceptible to no possible cure; when human nature and political institutions were seen to be corrupt as in the old countries; when in the course of a century Washington's peruque was all powder, Franklin's waistcoat all moths, and all of Jefferson leprosy; when, in the government's spirit the usurpation and shamelessness and impulse to attack its very essence, under the cloak of Liberty, both at home and abroad, and within the nation the same mania for public office, concerns, and the same improvidence that disfigure countries of less fortunate and grandiose completion—as if by magic there appeared a remedy upon every tongue; an apostle stood up in every pulpit as they did in the times of slavery; honored old men became enraged with youthful vigor; those same lances of the abolitionist crusade glistened; vigilant thinkers emerged from their silence, for, like the essence of the human body, they are the hidden essence of nations; and the Republic proved to be above its dangers.

So be it for the most important wrongs which are consuming the national spirit, all of them originating, like branches from a seed, from the exclusive cult of riches!   The country filled with reformers.   The campaign which began in the city election to deprive the vote-traders of power to elect the members of the municipalities to their liking, all-embracing shortly before, grew more rapidly than a rolling snowball, and in three years has started to attend to uprooting from those formidably organized traders the absolute and shameless dominion with which they were imposing their will, in the Presidential elections themselves, above the unanimous will of the nation and its most urgent necessities.

The campaign is digging down to the roots of the wrongs, and has seen where they originate. It is attacking them at their roots. Thus from time to time it is necessary to purge the field of worms and weeds.

Timidly at first, and then more energetically because of being rebuffed, a clamor for reform commenced to rise among the Republicans—reform in the method of appointing employees,[8] in

8. Marti is referring to the clamor for Civil Service Reform under which many offices in the government would be filled by competitive examinations rather than appointment by political bosses and other politicians.

electoral work and the collecting of funds for it, in the fraudulent distribution of Treasury surplus, in import duties which—being higher than the government requires for its expenditures—maintained active desires in the string of profiteers congregated in Washington to distribute that surplus among themselves; import duties which stimulated production of imperfect articles that were unsalable outside the country, not exportable, and every day made work scarcer, living costs higher, and the national problem more dismal. At first confronting the Democrats, later nearer to them, and finally at their side, the honest Republicans united in the demand for reforms. In some cases, they even originated and brought them about more energetically than the Democrats themselves, as in the law that establishes the election of junior employees in a national competition, and their promotion on the basis of merit. And since changing the system of granting positions was tantamount to beheading the Republican organization, there the aforementioned discord culminated, and there it turned into a war to the death. It was a mortal struggle between the Republicans who maintained the urgency of reforming the tariff, purifying the administration, and hindering, by a good employment system, the complicity of the government and the public functionaries in their violent and undue preservation of power—and those other more influential and numerous Republicans who, aided by the capitalists whose enterprises they favor, bring about their influence and well-being, and enable them to continue exercising their privilege of distributing positions among their friends and assistants.

Who was to be victorious in the Convention of the party's delegates, selected among those who subsist from its favor by those who share or expect it, if not those who hand out the benefits? Seconded by the capitalists, Blaine was the head of this faction— Blaine, who calls his intimates by their first names: the Joseph Joes, the Michaels Mikes, the Thomases Toms, and the Johns Johnnies, which leaves those goose-like people quite filled with flattery. Blaine, who talks with ruffians in their own jargon, with Irishmen against England, and Englishmen against Ireland. It was Blaine who tried to hold Peru[9] mortgaged (under American guarantees and power) to paying the claim of an adventurer with

9. The incidents referred to occurred during the war between Chile and Peru while Blaine was Secretary of State under President Arthur.

whom he would drink and talk, and whose interests he watched over so zealously that he turned a United States Cabinet member—who later died of shame—into a private agent for the claim, a man who abused his country's great name so that the belligerants would recognize the shady obligation. Blaine, fickle and unruly, extremely perspicacious and redoubtable but never great. Blaine, accused by evidence and by his own written confession, of having spontaneously and intentionally, in anticipation of being recompensed by shares, used his authority as Speaker of the House of Representatives so that it would vote a law which unduly favored the interests of a railroad in which he—for services no less criminal—already held a good part.[10] Blaine, who did not talk about putting his own house in order, but about entering the houses of others, to seek, on the pretext of trade accords and peace treaties, the wealth of which the Republican Party's economic mistakes have started to deprive the nation. Marketable Blaine, who, like he sells himself, buys and sells in the market of men. Such a convention nominated such a candidate. Blaine was the chosen one. Beneath the rented flags, and from among the treacherous delegates who had aided the victory, those who with generous expectations had come to the Convention to see an honest man nominated, filed out, blushing and filled with anger.

Meanwhile, the Democratic Party had commenced grooming itself for victory, which disasters nourish. Yet one cannot disregard the fact that the Democratic Party, even if apparently coinciding with the Republican Party in all serious questions, and even in its inner divisions, survived after having opened a road to the rebels by giving them some eminent supporters, and then continuing the war with the unanimous vote of the Union's enemies, that party carries within it a most powerful essence, and something akin to the substance of the Republic.

But the Federalists[11] had disseminated like today's Republicans, and the victorious Republicans failed to bring an essential body of

10. A decision of James G. Blaine while he was Speaker of the House of Representatives saved a land grant for the Little Rock and Fort Smith Railroad in 1869. In return Blaine received from the railroad managers the privilege of selling bonds on a commission that was secret.

11. The Federalist Party, organized in 1787, was generally viewed as representing the conservative interests of the planters, merchants,

doctrine, merely the temporal and accidental mission of keeping
together the Union, for whose defense they had been born. The
Democratic Party remained alive as the party of opposition, and
therefore has some legitimate and useful reasons to exist as the
ultimate symbol and nucleus of law of the rebel States' doctrine;
for it was only through that party that those States declared themselves. The Democratic Party, facing a transitory and infantile one,
was like a noble wooden vessel—trampled underfoot by guns, eaten
away by worms, burned by gun-powder—that guards the aromas of
those colossal flowers of justice and radiant thoughts by which this
nation came to life. That great family of States which had its in-
gratitude and turbulence like all young houses, but which then
settled down with the respect and punctilious courtesy of Puritan
homes; that basic and substantial eloquence, an absolute novelty and
a reflowering of the human mind, whose radiant paragraphs resemble
victory flags, and to which the grateful spirit appears as if to a
father's hand or to a new sea; that noble epic which will appear in
its own time when distance will permit it to be seen in proportion,
not defeating men but shaping them; not tinged in blood by some
lewd girl, like the epic of classical peruques, but by the ruins of
Man, who was poorly made the first time, recreating the human
creature and removing his restraints and crowning him with light;
that spirit, that letter, that revelation of the American people's
heroic times—all are perpetuating themselves like family traditions
which were usually left to the gray-haired Democratic Party, that
enjoys the prestige of legend and of a good home. Those accumula-
tions of virtue command respect. Men who throw stones at virtue
know that they need it to be saved.

It is in the posterity of illustrious personages that people see
the shadows of great men, as it were. And nations as well as children
love their parents more after they are dead. As soon as the war
was over, and the mercenaries whom the war permitted to survive
began to shine with the insolence and noise characteristic of the
upstarts, the people's eyes returned, as if to a breathing spell, to
that old, cornered, and expelled party which was purging its ostenta-
tion and errors in poverty; but in which—rather than in the brave

bankers, and manufacturers. Among its outstanding leaders were
George Washington, Alexander Hamilton, John Adams, and John Jay.
It was opposed by the Democratic-Republic Party led by Thomas
Jefferson and James Madison.

and victorious soldiers—the spirit of the Republic, in its black velvet suit and silver-buckled shoes, was still alive.

Before the war the South had been Democratic; defeated in its attempt to create its own nation, it kept its affiliation with the party that owed its rather ignominious departure from power to its compliance with the South as much as to its administrative corruption, which was as great as that of today's Republicans.

And since a considerable number of Democrats of the North had loyally served the Union's cause, it did not greatly harm them that the rebel States continued to be affiliated with them. On the contrary, it gave them a formidable mass of voters whom they needed to balance that of the Republicans, masters of the entire North, while adherence by the South was explained as the natural support of oppressed States to the party that maintained the national obligation of respecting, like another's wealth, the States' rights recognized by the Constitution. The Republicans were masters of the North, the Democrats masters of the South. The North was more densely populated than the South, but the Democrats were compensating their scanty population by means of their numerous partisans from the North. The battle, then, started from the first elections, and without words. With a slight slackening of Republican support, and a slight increase in that of the Democrats, the victory could change sides.

For a change in government there was no necessity for a definitive overturning of public opinion, merely a slight vacillation. For the Democrats, the contest was reduced to awaiting Republican mistakes, a calming down of the distrust in which they were held because of their traditional support in the rebel States, and presenting a more secure program for the great national issues than that of the Republicans, and in conformity with tradition. All of which they failed to do for quite some time, because they were blinded by local interests. And today the Democrats are regaining strength—not from within themselves or from any particular virtue of the Democratic idea, but from the confidence which Cleveland inspires in spite of his party, because of his independence and honesty, in a moment of a governmental corruption and national alarm in which independence and honesty are greatly needed.

74

Since the essential liberties without whose complete enjoyment peace is not justified in any honorable country were now assured; and since the rash attempt at separation—which endangered the Republic's efficiency as a form of government, and the existence of national union, both at the same time—had been defeated; since trusts and credits as a result of the war created enormous interests because of the population—the problems which followed the war, except the problem of southern franchises which the Republicans curtailed and the Democrats supported, were economic rather than political. The issue of major importance, and the only issue over which one of the two parties would have been able to fight, was the problem of free trade, which seemed to become the bone of contention in each election, but from which, as from some difficulty in which they could founder, both parties fled with equal tenacity.

Free trade—which only impedes the development of fictitious industries, and assures low general living costs, a stable base for wealth and commerce, and the peace that comes to the nation from this—was becoming less and less easy in the United States, because under the protection of a deceptive system, numerous violent industries have been created, employing hundreds of thousands of laborers whom both humanity and wisdom advise not to be suddenly left without work.

In the United States there are no parties of diverse classes vying for government. There are factory owners and laborers with the Democrats, and factory owners and laborers with the Republicans. The Democrats are outstanding for their noteworthy principles and self-sacrificing service to national affairs, but many of them are wealthy like Cox, and great factory owners like Hewitt.[12]

Both factory owners and laborers, as much from one party as from the other—according to their intellectual capacities and the independence of their industries—are either free traders or protectionists. So this could not be the dividing line between the rival parties. The Democratic Party has a powerful free trade branch: the Republican Party may have an even more powerful one. And

12. Abram S. Hewitt (1822-1903), industrialist and political leader. Hewitt made the first American-produced steel. He was a member of Congress (1875-1876, 1881-1886). He was elected mayor of New York City in 1886 as the Tammany-Democratic candidate. His reform policies led to a break with Tammany Hall and his defeat for re-election.

when one or another of these two contending opinions in the bosom of each party desired to exert itself to the utmost and be declared the party's dogma, the rival opinion has opposed it so energetically that the attempt has been abandoned, for it certainly would have split the party in two, and the party had to preserve its unity for its other purposes. In economics, then, both parties were equally vacillating. In religion, aside from the fact that both of them are being undermined by the Catholic Church as if by an otter's teeth, one is as divided between Catholics and Protestants as the other. In politics the different concepts of the nation and its government do indeed divide them, although they are unaware of it. For the Republicans, who came from the war, brought the victors' lack of restraint and aggressiveness to the conduct of national affairs, and in their politics they were always noted—like a hairy chest unable to be hidden by a shiny shirt bosom—by the traits of combat: spoils and violence; whereas the Democrats, who have been guarding the legend of the Republic, for a long time, were grudgingly watching the violent and novel crowds who are fond of pomp and imperial command, and of excursions into foreign countries, and who, because they had saved the nation from one danger, thought they were authorized to curse and dispense with its spirit. For this reason, although the guardians of the Republic—hostile to the soldiers—were unhappy with the many coarse immigrants who were followers of their preaching of liberties, they were moving over to the Democratic side.

But since apart from this distinction (invisible except to penetrating eyes) both govern equally abusively wherever they govern, for both are slices of the same people; since upon no major question did they differ, but were divided equally; since the only imposing problem, unless it were that of electoral and administrative corruption, was that of the economic system which exuberant production and trade difficulties were smothering—apparently both parties were to end by having to face that problem, and the free trade advocates, Republicans and Democrats, would go to one side, and the protectionists of both parties to the other.

But wealthy nations, conservative by their very nature, accept radical solutions only in extreme cases, and regard all changes with secret horror. And since at the same time as these economic difficulties whose remedy must necessarily be violent and costly—there was displeasure with the Republican arrogance, proofs of its imprudence in managing Treasury funds, and fear that electoral freedom, now much disfigured by those who have made a business of politics, might remain definitively in its hands—the unhappy nation's uneasiness and angers have appeared first here, because here the change has cost nothing.

And this, not by a jolt of the voting masses who shudder only when the sword pierces their flesh or the wolf howls at their door, but by the vigorous attack of thoughtful people who, as soon as they were certain of the Republic's peril, leaped upon platforms, delivered speeches from railroad trains, spread alarm throughout the nation, lined up their soldiers at the type cases, and won the contest by a split hair. But the curious thing is that the Democrats' victory was won by the Republicans.

The nation was being governed by the Republicans; but in some States by the Democrats, and in Democratically inclined New York, where opinion fluctuates, by both parties. This made it possible to see that those of the opposition were no more scrupulous in how they recruited supporters and rewarded them than those of the government. New York especially was being gnawed by a throng of obese and oily men dedicated, to their great advantage, to keeping the city's vote restricted to the interests of an old Democratic institution, "Tammany Hall."[13] By meting out small positions and inflaming Irish passions, it directed the city's vote, which is more important than that of the rest of the State and determines it. This institution not only imposed its candidates upon the party, but, because of New York's weight in national affairs, and because there can be no President without New York's vote, no Democratic Presidential candidate could appear unless he had consented beforehand to serve the interests of Tammany Hall. And it was a known fact that the candidates whom it managed to have elected entered their public offices obliged to share their posts and profits with members of Tammany Hall. From these more important positions it

13. Tammany Hall was originally the political headquarters of the Society of Tammany, also known as the Columbian Order, founded in 1783 as a political and benevolent society, but which later became a major symbol of corruption in government.

obtained the lesser ones by which it held the voters in subjection—voters who, in exchange for those posts, gave it the necessary power to impose conditions upon the men who desired to be selected, or to elect, by defeating their contenders, those whom the association desired to select.

Tammany Hall, being Democratic, for which reason we insist upon describing it, was a perfect example of that system of wardens, ring-leaders, political bosses of the vote who—by refusing to admit to the lists of the party's neighborhood associations anyone but those who respected its wishes—held the public vote in complete subjection. In the end those not admitted, who either out of indifference or respect regarded this abuse in silence, rebelled and voted. The revolt was in the Republican Party. The outraged voters rose up against the "boss," the ring-leader. The uprising first occurred in Brooklyn, home of the Protestant Church which, despite its narrow-mindedness—why not say so?—is guarding the seed of human liberty. Ah, Holland! Ah, William of Orange! Ah, planters! Your hands, discerning as a consecration, are still seen upon the shoulders of these reclaimers of the integrity of suffrage.

You brought human dignity to the cheek better than anyone in England or France, and it will never leave the face. Brooklyn was the first to rise up against the "boss" who was represented most perfectly in Tammany Hall. And that city elected as its mayor a rich and honest young man[14] over the opposition of the Brooklyn vote supervisors. Since the wrong was on a national scale, happiness spread throughout the country, and the growth of strength that brings victory spread among the voters. Then the State elected its governor over the head of the "boss." And finally, over the head of the "boss"—typified in Blaine—the nation elected its President.

The fabric of all that electoral scheming, the germ of all that vileness, was the distribution of public offices. Persons who "worked" for a party's victory proclaimed themselves, with exclusive right, to be recompensed by the party with the nation's offices, just as those who in some way contributed to the victory, and swelled the vote without recourse to influence or money,

14. Martí is referring to Seth Low.

believed that they were naturally entitled to the concessions and preferences which are in the hands of the administrators of national affairs. Therefore it was concluded that a man elected to some post, since he would not have obtained it without those self-serving votes, was nothing more in that post, than an accomplice and express servant of those interests. Evidently the nation was sold to the active traffickers in politics who, by removing impartial voters or those hindered by the worries of partisans or lukewarm persons from the ballot boxes, dominated the deliberations of both parties without a counter-weight. For where the Democrat arrived at government, since he had to climb the same tortuous ladder, he was subject to the same compromises. The government has posts to hand out, abuses to permit, and contracts to authorize; and the "workers" assumed that role because of their inordinate desire for positions, and their assistants because of their eagerness for contracts and licenses. That which irritated the good Republicans also irritated the good Democrats. And so both groups concurred in the salutory uprising.

Because that very difference in the ruling party between the full-blooded Republicans—who in all their extremes maintained boss politics in discipline, attack, and spoils, in the subservience of their opponents, in the mockery and ravaging of weak nations, and in a government of conquest upon conquest both at home and abroad—and the Half-Breed Republicans—who desired greater respect for the national will, less boasting in foreign relations, more integrity in elections and in the distributions of positions, more freedom for party members—that very difference also existed, for equal reasons and with the same ill-will, between the Democrats. Nobody here talks about the South whose symbolic democracy is divided due to local war-related reasons, but they do talk about the North, New York especially, where the wrongs were carried to an extreme, and the healing process has begun.

Among the Democrats, the old men who governed before the war were called "Bourbons"[15]—men who following the initial example

15. "Bourbon Democrats" were largely identified with intransigent pro-southern policies in the pre-Civil War period, and extreme upholders of slavery. The phrase was revived in the post-Civil War period to refer to the reestablished southern advocates of "white supremacy," who were held to be behind the times and unteachable.

of the days of ardent strife, could not conceive of an administration employing anyone who failed to share its political views; men who contracted in government the vices which originated in it and corrupted the Republicans; men who desired to return to national government for the sake of the Democrats, rather than for the sake of the nation, and who stood for tradition, not for the times. But in these twenty years, many right-thinking persons, many guardians of national liberty, many young people whose faces were made to blush by Republican haughtiness, many voters from the North who saw risks of war or repression in the Republican Party's tendency to bring together in federal power the authorities that belong to the United States and guarantee the balance and reform which are indispensable to the existence of this vast and populous nation—all these persons had joined the Democratic Party, as the only fighting party besides the one in government, and created within it new fabrics, as it were, free from the moths that threatened the preoccupied minds and short silk jackets of the powdered "Bourbons." Neither the jealousies of the North, nor the invasions of Mexico,[16] neither petty intolerance, nor governmental exploitation to benefit the followers. Facing the wrongs created by the Republican Party, and because they disliked them, these new people under the Democrats had banded together not to fight like the "Bourbons" to regain their influence and make good use of it, but rather to destroy Republican abuses; to stem the immoral thirst for public posts as far as possible; to establish party organizations so that all their members might freely express and carry out their desires within those organizations; to reform the elections so that the functionaries would not be merely executors of the wishes of the cliques who assured them of their appointments; to relieve imported articles and life in general of unnecessary taxes, without suddenly compromising the condition of the established industries; and moreover to remove from the Treasury coffers the exploiters

16. On April 25, 1846, after many diplomatic disputes and negotiations, the Mexicans entered the disputed territory between the Nueces and Rio Grande rivers into which U. S. General Zachary Taylor had moved his troops in July 1845 even though there was ample evidence that they were encroaching on Mexican territory. Calling this an invasion of U. S. territory, President James K. Polk, who had been waiting for the opportunity, requested a declaration of war against Mexico, which Congress passed on May 12, 1846. After losses in battles, the Mexicans surrendered. On February 13, 1848, the Treaty of Guadalupe-Hidalgo was concluded, terminating hostilities. Under the peace terms, Mexico surrendered about half of its territory to the United States.

who misuse them. It is against these new Democrats that the job seekers, the merchants who aid and manage them, and the "Bourbons" clamor.

The "Bourbons" are disciplinarians, and want control as their birthright, from which nothing is owed to those who are not party members, and in this they are like full-blooded Republicans. The new Democrats view the government as a way of affirming their own profit by impartially serving general national interests, and they do not believe that the government is a grange of members of the victorious party where they can even pick the fruit and plunder at will, but as a warehouse, and in this they are like Half-Breed Republicans.[17] Therefore the best of the Republicans and the best of the Democrats came with similar spirit, talking within their party with similar enemies and brought close by natural congeniality. Timidly at first, and like a test, they met in Buffalo to elect Cleveland mayor of the city. Now more frankly, although not confessing it publicly, they again gathered their resources together to elect Cleveland, always Cleveland, as governor of New York State. Finally openly, and in notorious rebellion, many of the most illustrious delegates left the Republican Convention; they decided to support the Democratic candidate, and did so, if in view of this support he would be, as he always was, Grover Cleveland.

Because the Democratic Party had the good fortune to have a reformer required by the times appear within its ranks: a man hard as a mallet, sound as an apple, independent as a stallion. Neither in language nor in life is he pompous. When a scoundrel passes by, he says: "Oh, that fellow." When he is asked to do what he must not do, he says: "No!" When he is shown that some act of justice will harm his personal advancement or that of his party, he says: "It's fair." And since the country is now afraid the abusers are drying up its wealth even more than the "workers" are vitiating its political liberties, everyone has dedicated himself to supporting this unpretentious man who has fearlessly stood up for cleaning out the scoundrels and watching over the money chests.

17. A term of contempt applied by former Radical Republicans who favored a conciliatory policy to the South after 1877, advocated Civil Service reform, opposed the spoils system, and fought against corruption in the Republican Party.

With the aid of such upright Republicans, and against the Bourbonian sentiments of his Party, Cleveland was elected mayor of Buffalo, to govern it impartially and independently. He conducted the city's affairs with such integrity, and won such fame for this, that the Democratic Party's younger element put him triumphantly ahead of the vanquished "Bourbons" as candidate for the governorship of New York State, to which post he ascended upon the shoulders of the Democrats and Republicans who assisted him either with their abstention because their party's candidate failed to please them, or with their silent vote. And since Cleveland in his extremely difficult post showed that he knew how to reconcile the gratitude toward his voters with his duties to the State, since he did not have to pay for a position which he had not solicited; since he was elected in spite of Bourbonism-filled Tammany Hall, and acceded neither to the desire to attract more Republican wills nor to the threats of Tammany Hall; since he governed with his party without being unfaithful to his duties to the nation, but rather to its advantage and in an exemplary manner, as he ought to in days when there was a clamor for honesty and strength—Cleveland's fame as a strong and honest man increased.

Naturally, when both the Republican scorn for public opinion, and the indignation of the nation, culminated due to the Republican Convention's nomination of Blaine as its candidate for the Presidency, the yearning for reforms in the man who had shown no fear to implement them, nor any exaggeration with which to discredit them, nor weakness in carrying them to a conclusion—Grover Cleveland— also reached a climax in the Democratic Convention.

The dissident Republicans, considering Blaine's nomination a slap in the face, organized in the States, assembled in a public meeting, proclaimed their determination to vote with the Democrats and, against a great part of the Democrats themselves, made them emerge the victors.

Those who were most bitten by Bourbonism, the liveliest supporters of the old-time Democrats, those who did not want any young Democrats in the government (men shaped by present-day problems to save the nation) but wanted the old-time Democrats who were unconditional friends of their henchmen and devoted to their service; the ballot box ring-leaders who had filled **Tammany** Hall, and whom Cleveland always treated with utmost severity and without that adulation to which the suffrage solicitors have accustomed the Tammany Hall people—all the foregoing turned against Cleveland in a body, and whether in secret or openly, dispensed with their vote or gave it to Blaine, who found easy followers among these Irish "Toms" and "Mikes" and was aided by them, in exchange of the promise—contradicted by his previous conduct—that, in defense of the Irish, he was going to lay hands upon the English neck as upon a bulldog.

Tammany Hall has much influence upon New York voters, and has them very well organized. Many Tammany votes were doubtless absent on election day, although in public the Hall said that it would support Cleveland, and then went on to celebrate his inauguration in Washington. Many of the Irish voted for Blaine, although many Germans, until now Republicans, voted with the Democrats. But New York City's other Democratic associations to which the Presidential battle was reduced, given the national bipartisan balance of forces; the business interests in a body that filled the rainy streets with parades and flags; the dissident Republicans who upon platforms, in pulpits, and press fought for Cleveland with an ardor that cooled down many of the irate "Bourbons" among the Democrats, and were finally, not without utmost difficulty, able to surpass the vote of the disciplined Republicans and the turncoat Democrats by little more than one million out of ten million ballots; honest votes, wings of the law, besides the blameworthy although perspicacious candidacies such as Butler's,[18] or ineffective such as that of the Temperance Party,[19] or curious like that of the lady favored by the Women's Suffrage Societies[20]—all these have carried the unpretentious reformer—to air and purify it—to the White House!

18. Benjamin F. Butler was the candidate of the Anti-Monopoly and Greenback parties.

19. The Prohibition Party, formed by the Temperance movement, conducted its first presidential campaign in 1872. Its greatest success was obtained in 1892 when it polled 271,000 votes. It advocated prohibition of the manufacture and sale of intoxicating liquors.

20. The reference is to Belva Ann Lockwood (1830-1917), lawyer and the first woman to practice before the U. S. Supreme Court (1879), who was nominated in 1884 by the National Equal Rights Party for the presidency of the United States. She was again nominated in 1888.

Thus did the Republican Party fall from power: thus does the youthful element of the Democratic Party rise, and remain in power under those difficulties. Virtue has no more irritated enemies than those who see it close at hand.

JOSÉ MARTÍ

La Nación, Buenos Aires, May 9, 1885

To the Editor of *La Nación:*

The elections are at the height of their ardor: gubernatorial elections in several States, as well as those of judges and mayors.

All through the summer the politicians have been marshalling their forces to defeat their opponents in the winter contests, beginning in September with the battle of the ballot boxes.

When August gilds the ripened fields, heated passions begin to line up for the Autumn elections; since these are local, they are always fought tooth and nail, with formidable hatred. Here, people debate the way they box, in a ring and without gloves. In our lands, all our clothing would soon be drenched in blood if we heard those things which are calmly accepted in this country. Some improvement has been made in that regard, but only in the important cities, just as in a house better care is taken of the parlor than of the back rooms.

There in the midwestern States, votes are bought and sold just as in New York; but the language and accusations are shocking in their boldness and perversity.

For fifty dollars one governor buys votes from the delegates to the convention called to nominate the party's candidate.

Another offers a pardon to criminals in the penitentiary, and at night lets his own secretary into the place to have the prisoners affirm, under written oath, that during the Democratic government they were obliged to flay the Irish and Negroes who were dying in

the prison "and make walking canes out of pieces of their skin."
Incredible?

Yet the one saying this is Ohio's Republican governor Foraker,[1]
who goes from rostrum to rostrum reading the sworn statements
in public.

"Not only that," he adds, "but the Democratic governor hired
a Prison Warden who was receiving money from the prisoners, from
inmate Banley, to be well treated and given easy work." "You're
lying!" cries one of the audience from the bench: "Here is a copy
of your letter to the Warden, who's my friend":

"Mr. Warden, I shall thank you to take convict Hiram Banley
out of the contract gang, and place him in some other. Governor
Foraker." But this defeat fails to discourage the candidate; two
hours later, he delivers another speech. His arguments seem to be
firmer than those involving the Warden and the flayed prisoners:
"There is no fraud that the Democrats haven't committed in the
Ohio elections; they've registered people who have no right to
vote; the same men voted twice; ballots that nobody cast appeared
in the ballot boxes, and the Republican ballots would vanish; those
in charge of the counting did so disloyally, and swore falsely. Who
in Ohio is not aware of this? That election was a farce, a true
robbery. And the judges? When we went to the courts, there was
always a Democratic judge ready to approve the fraud."

This is truly not one of Foraker's dreams; that is how the
Republicans here snatched the Presidency from Tilden;[2] that is how
Blaine's friends in the last Presidential campaign tried to steal it
from Cleveland; that is how the municipal elections here are usually
perverted: by falsifying registration lists and manipulating the
ballot boxes.

1. Joseph Benson Foraker (1846-1917), Republican governor of Ohio
   (1885-1890), U.S. Senator (1897-1909), leader of the "Old Guard" of the
   Republican Party.

2. The reference is to the Election of 1876, known as the "Disputed
   Election" in which Rutherford B. Hayes, the Republican candidate for
   president, defeated Samuel J. Tilden, the Democratic candidate. The
   election was decided by an Electoral Commission appointed by both
   houses of Congress, which gave the election to Hayes by one vote.
   The deciding vote was cast by a Republican.

Do you want a sample of the language, the governor's language? Well, this how Governor Foraker talks in his electoral speeches: "All Democratic employees are a string of incapable incompetents, shameless daring scoundrels who have been robbing and plundering right and left from the day they rose to power till they were kicked out of it in order to be where they deserve, waiting to be ordered, as they must be, to purge their crimes by serving the State—not as office holders but in the penitentiary."

That describes Ohio. In Connecticut, where a governor is also being elected now, the candidate is accused of having obtained the Republican Convention's votes with money.

Is he being accused by a Democrat, or some no-account person, or one of those salaried dogs who bark or lick for pay? No. The accuser, author of a detailed brochure, is a most important Republican in his city.

But this seems to stem from the deep division within party ranks; when they work together, everything seems sacred to them; when their obligations or passionate support for opposing leaders divide them, they accuso their former friends of crimes which they themselves have committed.

Neither charity nor the white glove are natural products of the United States. Blaine persecutes his enemies with neither charity nor white gloves, just as he himself is persecuted.[3] Even his hair, which hangs in unruly wisps over his forehead, reveals the implacable emotion of his politics. In this aggressive and combative country his rare aggressiveness dazzles and inspires love even in his enemies. His versatility, catholicity, and genuinely forceful language, enliven the fascination felt by men most of whom are lacking in it. And even in Blaine's defects, in the skillful sale of his political influence, in the imperturbable ease with which he confronts the gravest and most thoroughly proved accusations, in his stubborn decision to put his person, with all manner of skills, over and above

3. This is probably a reference to attacks on various political figures by Blaine in his *Twenty Years in Congress* (2 vols., 1884-1886), a widely-read autobiography.

those who stand in his way, in his evident lack of scruples and modesty in committing and concealing his public faults—most of the country's masses seem to be watching and pardoning themselves in him, for they see in that triumphant political sinner a ratification of their own unbridled love of success.

Furthermore, he has the tact to see in what direction his country's momentary emotion is going; and with the magnificent leaps of a tiger, he puts himself at the head of it. Nothing depresses him. Nothing discourages him. And that astounding ability to survive, that ardent and indomitable faith in himself and in his luck, assure him of the admiration of and the power over the great masses—in a country, made up of men who see life as a field of conquest, and who calmly attack the clergymen's pulpits, the attorney's banks, and the political forum—if things go badly on their pig farms or in their shoe stores. That flexible man represents this resilient country well.

The gubernatorial election in the State of Connecticut this year is only one episode in Blaine's drama. The day after his casual defeat by Cleveland, he got up out of the dust, wiping the perspiration from his face, with a frightful speech upon his lips, his candidacy once again within his grasp.

Ever since that very instant, cold ran in the marrow of the Republicans, who, because of honesty or envy, had aided in his overthrow. His valiant tenacity kept his friends at his side at the moment when, believing that he was finished politically, they were preparing to abandon him.

Not one friend did he lose after his defeat. He spied with relish upon the Democratic Party's unhappy discussions, its inability to reach an agreement upon questions of silver, the tariff, and public offices; upon the resistance of the interested masses of the Party to help Cleveland with the reform policies to which he owes his eminence, upon the Attorney General's complicity in a private telephone company, and upon the mistakes committed by Secretary Bayard[4] in the Mexican case.

4. Thomas Francis Bayard (1828-1898), U.S. Senator from Delaware (1869-1885); U.S. Secretary of State in the Cleveland administration (1885-1889).

It is not true that both Democrats and Republicans are accusing him of having sold his influence and authority as Speaker of the House of Representatives for shares in a railroad company?[5] Well, here the Democratic Attorney General uses his secretarial influence and authority, as well as funds from the national Treasury, for his own interests and those of a private company! Were not both Republicans and Democrats saying that he had dishonored the State Department with a shameless policy of haggling in the countries of America? Well, here is the Democratic Secretary of State precipitating an odious war against Mexico to assure a greater number of southern State followers of his candidacy to the Presidency!

Blaine has made capital of all this for the ardent campaign of his latest candidacy.

His army is in order; his friends obey him blindly; his voice this Autumn has been enough to prevent the Republicans in his own State of Maine from being defeated by the Temperance Party; his lieutenants are ordered not to permit any Republican hostile to Blaine's candidacy to the Presidency of the Republic to raise his head.

He is fighting with a sword, and his enemies are fighting him with swords. That is why it is a notable Republican hostile to Blaine who accuses of bribery and corruption—with facts—the Blainist Republican candidate for governor of Connecticut. It is through State governments that one reaches the Presidency.

By eyeing these lesser elections, we are involuntarily studying the great Presidential election of 1888.

When Blaine was chosen as his party's candidate in the past election, his most respected and upright colleagues, who abandoned him, were praised by the public. They reiterated with proofs the patent

5. The reference is to the role of Blaine, then Speaker of the House, in the sale to the Union Pacific Railroad of certain securities at prices higher than their value. This scandal was revealed in "The Mulligan Letters," written by Blaine to James Mulligan, a former clerk of a Boston business house. In these letters written by Blaine from 1869 on, the Speaker of the House discussed with Mulligan the disposition of Union Pacific securities at prices higher than their value. Revelations about the letters in 1884 contributed heavily to Blaine's defeat as a presidential candidate.

charges brought against his personal and political honesty, and without departing from Republican Party doctrine, worked for Cleveland's election as "independents," against the Democrats themselves, preferring in national government an upright adversary to a blemished colleague.

And now, for 1888, the situation seems to be the same. By all that has been seen until today, Blaine is gathering together more votes and more enthusiasm in his party than the stern Edmunds,[6] verbose Logan,[7] and the cautious Sherman.[8] And the pure Republicans appear to be ready to keep the Democrats in government rather than contribute to giving power to a guilty politician who, in their judgment, dishonors the Republican Party.

But it is not in Maine where the most curious event of the Autumn campaign is taking place, although Blaine has waged some brilliant battles there against the Temperance Party, which is very powerful in that puritanical region. Neither is it in Connecticut where one Republican is denouncing another who has bought, dollar by dollar, the convention that nominated him, and is making use of Church influence in this election to substantiate this robbery which is unworthy of the public vote. It is not even in Ohio where the governor himself asserts that in the official prison walking canes were being made out of Irishmen's and Negroes' skin.

The most curious event is in Tennessee, where two brothers, one a Republican and the other a Democrat, travel across the State together as rival candidates for the gubernatorial post, each one defending his own party in a continuous debate from the same stage.

They talk from the same rostrum: sleep under the same roofs, each one imposing upon his friends a personal respect for his

6. George Franklin Edmunds (1828-1919), U.S. Senator from Vermont (1866-1891).

7. John Alexander Logan (1826-1886), Union Army general and Republican Senator from Illinois (1871-1877; 1879-1886). Logan ran for vice-president with Blaine as the presidential candidate, but was defeated.

8. John Sherman (1813-1900), U.S. Senator from Ohio (1861-1877; 1881-1897), Secretary of the Treasury (1877-1881), Secretary of State (1897-1898).

brother; they debate the merits and shortcomings of their respective parties, without restraint and swept by passion. Towns welcome them; parades follow them; they deliver speeches in theaters, woods, and grottos; magnificent cavalcades accompany them; at the end of every debate they are covered with flowers. Young Democratic women leave their towns to welcome their candidate Bob Taylor, all of them dressed in white with a white rose adorning their breasts. Throughout the campaign Alf and Bob have not been apart for a single day; it is said that Tennessee has never had a more brilliant debate, and that despite their frankness in discussion, the respect with which the two brothers treat one another has divested this political campaign of its usual brutality.

The Tennessee residents have felt the romance of this event; and although on their day they will vote for the one who most nearly touches their souls or their pocketbooks, they are now glad to divide their affections equally between the two competing brothers.

Both play the violin, and—oh, the simplicity of budding nations! —one night after the discussion, each one was presented with a violin on the stage and, seated in their twin chairs, they continued to debate with some musical selections.

After his speech yesterday, Bob was given a violin made out of spikenards.

These two men, sons of a peaceable Protestant minister, are extremely eloquent. Short and solidly built Alf, the Republican, has his big head crammed with facts and the ability to reason. Tall Bob, the Democrat, has magnetic charm, hands that hold fast what he touches, eyes that make friends, and a fighting, sparkling expressiveness. Alf releases his sentences with the skill of a target shooter; he aims, cherishing the target, strikes where it hurts, but never arouses passion. Bob's feathers are seen to be ruffled beneath his full dress coat; he seizes his brother's phrases in mid flight, like a fighting cock, not stopping until they are demolished. When his brother comes forth with a good argument, he lets it pass as if he were permitting him to emerge the winner; but he suddenly falls upon him with some amusing phrase; and the reasoning which he cannot answer, he kills with anecdotes, always a successful device with ignorant audiences.

Since a certain section of the State is Republican and another Democratic, it happened that in the Democratic section, a lout tried to insult Alf. Bob stood up, attacked the audience—which has no reputation for kindness in Tennessee—and said: "Whoever insults my brother insults me!" And the insults stopped.

Hurt at the height of a debate once, Alf turned grimly pale. "The only Democratic vote I've ever cast," he said with a quivering voice, "I cast for this thankless brother of mine! If he had been nominated candidate before me, I never would have permitted myself to be nominated later."

Bob reddened upon hearing this, but when the debate was finished that night, he took his brother peacefully by the arm.

"I love him, I love him as a person," said Alf three nights ago in the midst of his speech, turning to his brother, "but politically I despise him, despise him! I want the Negroes to be educated," he continued...

"First pay your debts, Republican!" one of Bob's followers interrupted from the audience.

"I'm sure," Alf responded, "that the person talking to me has never paid a debt himself!"

That is how they argue, night after night, from one city to another, about free trade which Bob wants and Alf does not; about Blair's bill[9] which Bob is against because he does not believe that the Negroes, who are free citizens of a State, should be educated with national funds, with federal charity.

The debate continues in the city streets, upon train seats, at the head of parades, in their private conversations.

Around them are always some attentive followers who collect their retorts and popularize them as the lesser election coinage in which Bob has the advantage. An elderly farmer approaches Bob:

9. The Blair bill called for the use of federal funds to further education of Negroes in the South. It was defeated in Congress.

"I have the right to greet you because thirty good Democrats were born from me: seven sons and twenty-two grandsons." *(sic)* "You haven't lived in vain, my good old man." "No wonder there are so many Democrats in Tennessee," whispered Alf.

Bob is handsome, much handsomer than Alf; but an elderly farmer, a staunch Republican, came to where the two were sitting, regarded them curiously, and finally turned to Alf, as if consoling him with his glance, and said: "You look the best to me, Alf."

That is how those rival brothers continue to travel from village to village in this singular campaign.

The entire State dresses in its Sunday best to go out to see them. Large crowds at the roadsides greet them when their train passes. The Republicans' wives display red handkerchiefs, the Democrats' wives white ones. Their respective supporters await them in separate rows at all the railroad stations, sometimes on horseback, to accompany them to the esplanade or the small woods nearby where the crowds can be accommodated; at other times on foot, to follow them from the station to the town hall or a theater.

And they move through the streets in two separate rows, on horseback or on foot, some with their white rose or ribbon on the lapels of their frock coats, others with a red rose, dahlia, or ribbon.

The women regale them with flags, banners, bouquets of flowers, and fine fruit.

The men argue over the honor of lodging them in their homes.

The Democratic gentleman who lodges both of them in his home, smiling at his wife on their way to the table, asks: "Which one will escort you?" "Both," she replies, and she walks on between the two, one brother on each arm, amid much applause.

That same night ten thousand Democrats crowded beneath the balconies of the house to serenade Bob. The entire street was a fireworks display of flags, torches, and roses. Surprised, Bob went out on the balcony. The crowds immediately realized that they might hurt his feelings with the serenade, by involuntarily leaving his brother humiliated; and at the top of their lungs, as though they were singing a hymn, they demanded to have both brothers come out!

But the true quality of that hymn is the energy and affection, the contagious and congenial faith with which the New York workers, united for the first time in a serious political effort, are trying to elect as mayor of this city of work one of the boldest, purest and clearest of thinkers, a man who today is fixing his attention upon the confused feelings of a new world: Henry George.[10]

With his Socratic bearing, he seems to be shedding some light upon this apostolic campaign.

The clergy are helping him, and so are the reformers who are like the clergy.

Many Latin Americans are helping him with their words and influence. The merely political parties are not hiding their fear in the face of the coming of this new force; and it is clear that the spirit of this city, product of deeds and capable of them, is respectfully receiving the candidacy of this honest innovator.

We are heedfully attending this baptism of a new race.

JOSÉ MARTÍ

La Nación, Buenos Aires, December 7, 1886

10. Henry George (1839-1897), celebrated author of *Progress and Poverty* (1879), which became one of the most widely read books on political economy in the United States and influenced many in Europe. George argued that land belongs to society, which created its value and that if it were properly taxed, through the "Single Tax," poverty could be eliminated. In the fall of 1886 George ran for Mayor of New York City on the United Labor Party ticket and was almost elected.

THE PRESIDENT'S MESSAGE. — ANTECEDENTS AND PRESENT STATE OF THE POLITICAL SITUATION. — EMERGENCE OF A NEW PARTY. — THE OPEN BATTLE BETWEEN THE PRESIDENT AND HIS PARTY CONTINUES. — THE DEMOCRATS LOSE GROUND. — THE GEORGISTS. — CONGRESS IS IN SESSION. — EXCERPTS FROM CLEVELAND'S MESSAGE. — MAIL SERVICES TO THE RIVER PLATTE INCREASE. — PEACE WITH MEXICO. — TARIFF REDUCTION. — POLITICAL SKILL OF THE MESSAGE. — THE FUTURE.

New York, December 8, 1886

To the Editor of *La Nación:*

With the first days of December in the United States there is always a renewal of political activity.

Congress is in session again. The President is defining his position in a message to it. The Secretaries' reports are detailing the state of their departments. The press of each party, or of one of its factions, is formulating its program.

People are eagerly awaiting the first actions of the Representatives and Senators gathered in Washington, in order to deduce from them the direction to be taken by national affairs.

It is not customary here to set forth each political group's situation, as in monarchic parliaments where there are speeches in response to the message from the Crown.

Restricted by their commitments and differences, the representatives shrink from precise and definitive formulas. The newspapers, which learn the direction of public opinion close at hand from their ledgers, take it upon themselves to reveal what is in people's minds, even if counter to their liking and predilections.

Today especially, neither of the two rival parties woud be able to define its policy in a fixed program, because the fact is that each of them is split up into enemy factions, together only for the need of mutual support to maintain or assault power.

The Republican Party—justly discredited for its mismanagement in government, for its arrogant intolerance, its system of excessive taxation, its bad distribution of the Treasury surplus and public

99

lands, its systematic falsification of the vote, its complicity in powerful companies, its scorn for majority interests—would doubtless have been unable to reestablish itself in power for a long time if the Democratic Party succeeding it had not demonstrated its confusion in matters of urgent resolution, its shortsightedness and indifference in the essential matters which are disquieting the nation, and its prevailing eagerness to take possession, like the Republicans, of public offices.

The Democratic Party was brought to the government, if not to carry out a precise program which its internal divisions prevented it from offering, at least to govern with a different spirit from the corrupting, absorbing, and awesome spirit of the Republicans—in order to cease doing those things for which the Republicans had drawn unanimous censure, even from their friends and founders. The Democratic Party was brought to the government to reform the tariff in a manner that would put production upon a profitable basis, without causing an immediate shake-up in industry, or leaving the workers unemployed. It was brought to power to reduce the unnecessary hundred million dollar surplus in the Treasury, thereby lowering the country's living cost by that amount, along with a consequent reduction of import duties; to facilitate a price reduction in industrial products by means of the free entry of raw materials and a salary reduction; and to remove from the reach of speculators and pilferers the surplus in the cash boxes—a surplus solicited with frivolous excuses for extravagant or immoral enterprises.

The Democratic Party was brought to the government to honestly discuss the desirability of continuing the minting of silver coins, which are not salable; to prevent the unreasonable cession of federal lands to powerful companies which take possession of the representatives' votes in exchange for gifts or protection. It was brought to the government in order to keep the government from becoming, as it was beginning to become, the exclusive and truly scandalous property of the wealthy cliques which—with the aid of the Secretaries and Representatives whom they corrupt, intimidate, or favor—were very hastily taking possession of the national wealth, of those in charge of distributing it, and of the methods and avenues, in the political structure, directed to assure the people of the knowledge and management of their interests and domains.

And it turns out that after two years of enjoying power, with the executive in its hands and with a majority in the House of Representatives, the Democratic Party has not reformed the tariff, has not honestly discussed the silver question, has not reduced the hundred million dollar surplus in the national Treasury, has given no signs of desiring the morality offended by the Republicans in the distribution and handling of public offices, and has not truly legislated with a spirit different from that of the Republicans.

It has been stated graphically here: "They can knock down a building, but they don't know how to make a spoon."

They can indeed destroy, but not build. Instead of reducing the surplus, the Democrats have tried to distribute it among themselves. They have committed the same abuses that they reviled in their rivals.

And they have shown some action and cohesion only to oppose the policies of their own President, to combat all proposals of his that lead to the purposes for which they were elected, and to force him, in payment for his party's benevolence, to distribute public offices within it, as the rights of victory.

In vain does the President—nominated to purify the system of public office allotments as a principal means of freeing suffrage from fraud, and cleansing the government—attempt to conciliate, with prudent concessions, the law that imposes competition and promotion in providing public offices, with the system of entirely changing them, from street sweepers to ministers, at every new election[1]—which causes the vice of serving the parties because of the profit expected from them, and the creation of a breed of traffickers in national posts—both things baneful for republics.

In vain does Cleveland—attentive to the country's voice, to its

1. The reference is to the Pendleton Act of 1883, the first significant Civil Service reform measure. The law established a bipartisan Civil Service Commission of three members charged with the duty of administering a partial merit system in the federal service. Under its provisions the federal service was to be partially classified into grades to which appointments were to be made on the basis of success in competitive examinations. The law also forbade political assessments on office holders or removal from office for failure to make voluntary contributions to political campaigns.

offerings, and to his own legitimate personal ambition—yield no more than that in which he can give in without dishonor, and insist upon asking his party to keep the promises which elevated him to power. These promises are tariff reform, elimination of the Treasury surplus, cessation of the minting of silver coins; making studies of the reforms needed for land distribution and for all the country's acute problems; studies of industry's fear of being unable to produce at low cost; of the restlessness of the workers whom prosperity fails to reach; of the offensively excessive accumulation of wealth by companies favored by Congressional laws and the gifts. The party also promised to make studies of building a strong fleet and coastal defense works, improve the condition of the Indian tribes, and implement an effective distribution to each individual of the land which today those tribes possess only nominally and in common.

In vain have the Democrats been defeated, as an alarming announcement that public opinion has been offended, in many electoral districts which have been discontented with their incompetence to implement from the government the improvements which they considered so dear when they disputed the Republicans' position.

In vain, out of so great an amount of true public alarm in questions of work and land abuse, is a party being formed in all haste with harmony, eloquence, and formidable determination, and ready to resolve those questions without violence but without delay.

As things have appeared until today, all is in vain. The Republicans, less visible now that they are out of power, are gradually trying to settle their differences, since they are not nourished by the conflicting appetites that aggravate them when their party is in government.

The Democrats—determined, as it is easy to see, not to deal peacefully with the President until he yields to them upon the principal public office issue—show no sign of agreeing upon questions on which the country impatiently awaits his action: the tariff, the surplus, and silver. Because in the question of public offices, the truth is that there is so little regard here for what does not directly concern the pocketbook, that it cannot be said that the country is showing true insistence upon the reforms which Cleveland is upholding with relative although meritorious zeal: thinkers were always in the minority.

The Democrats are throwing in each others' faces the cause of their recent losses in the Autumn elections; and while Cleveland's friends affirm with apparent logic that the reason for the defeat was the party's delay in promulgating the reforms for whose implementation it was elected, the President's adversaries respond that the Democrats have suffered that defeat because of Cleveland's hesitation in distributing public posts among his followers—as if confessing that interest were not enough to show the urgency of remedying such a vilification of political affairs!

"The defeat occurred because the tariff was not reformed," say the free traders. "The defeat was a censure on the endeavours to reform the tariff," say the protectionists.

But those were actually lesser reasons, although real ones. The principal reasons lay elsewhere.

The country is displeased with the lack of agreement, the egoism, indecision, excessive rivalry, narrowness of purpose, and lack of national soul revealed by the Democrats in their two years in government.

The poorly concealed resemblance of spirit and habits among the professional politicians, whether Republicans or Democrats, disenchants public opinion.

But above all, that spirit of reform—healthful and sudden as a stormy wind, which recurs periodically in United States history in every critical moment like the Springtime of liberty, a result of it, and a valve of the Republic—is actively threatening both parties. It is also apparent that this healthful spirit always comes from learned people—the Protestant clergy—and from simple-heartedness, from the multitudes who live in truth, shaped and hardened by work.

Profit creates worms. It is among the poor that the sincerity which drives the worms away prospers.

United States politics, then, is divided between two worn-out parties which are disorganized into factions maintained by personal jealousies and differences in ideas, and one emerging party[2] which is too new and radical for its coming to power to be counted as an immediate factor, although the old parties are already feeling upon their backs the lash which is beginning to give chase to them.

The Republicans seem incapable of uniting under a common program and leadership both Blaine's friends—who respond to his personal magic allowing him to keep the influence which might have made another less able and eloquent man lose his versatility, and what is more, his political immorality—and the friends of Edmunds, a staunch sectarian, but strongly attached to the honest and impartial old spirit of public liberty which Blaine's brilliant cynicism scorns and threatens.

And if anyone's stature increases and becomes predominant in the Republican Party, it is not Edmunds—who at Arthur's[3] funeral held out his hand to Blaine whom he had insulted—but Blaine, who refused to accept it.

The Democrats on their part, paying no attention to the evident approval with which Cleveland's honest and sensible conduct is received, every day prove to be angrier for not having been able to subject him to their will. They are encouraging opposition against the employment method and the President supports. They are responding to his abrupt honesty with annoyance and insults, are still as divided among themselves as if they were mortal enemies, and see nothing in Cleveland's popularity but a reason to accuse him of sacrificing his party's good for the sake of his own reputation.

2. The reference is to the United Labor Party, headed by Henry George, which continued as a state and national party for a few years after the election of 1886 in New York in which George was defeated for Mayor. George received 68,110 votes or 31 percent of the total votes cast. The winner, Abram S. Hewitt, obtained 90,552 or 41 percent of the total. Theodore Roosevelt ran third with 60,435 votes or 27.6 percent of the total. The feeling was widespread that George had been "grossly counted out."

3. Chester A. Arthur (1830-1886), New York Republican lawyer and politician, elected vice-president of the United States in 1880, and succeeded to the presidency on the death of James A. Garfield; held office until 1885.

The Georgists—who can be known as such because their leader is Henry George—the most brilliant and conspicuous group of those attempting reform, are spreading the ideas of legitimate democracy, of reform in present-day labor conditions, of transforming the land into public property, and uniting all contributions in one sole tax upon occupied land—aided by Protestant's liberal sects and by the simple-hearted Catholic clergy. Their doctrines are finding no reception in the powerful corporations which today are disposing of almost all productive wealth, nor in that portion of the Protestant and Catholic clergy who live near the rich and from them, and seem resolved to make a heavenly parapet of defense for them.

This new party is spreading, as if establishing roots, through the town councils of the large cities; sending representatives to the State legislatures and Congress; preaching actively throughout the country; organizing for maximum action upon precise bases, whether with the name of Progressive Democracy or the more frequent United Labor Party. It practices the customs of peace and respect for democracy, and now counts upon the powerful aid of the labor unions to such an extent that the entire country is giving an attentive ear to it, and Henry George is as much mentioned as a respectable candidate for a future Presidential race, as the men of note who later saved the Union at the head of the Republican Party were mentioned in the first "Friends of free land" campaigns.

There is undoubtedly an attempt now being made to see how, by paying attention to the just complaints in time, the country can be saved from a social war.

Congress has met in these battle conditions.

The President has sent it his message in which the ink is still wet—a bold and stable ink which leaves no doubt about what he is saying.

The message is explicit, moderate, and sincere. It contains neither generalities nor pomp! This President understands his position as the administrative office which it is, and which must give an account to the owners of what he administers.

In the new heterogenous countries, which are in one or another way primitive, a President can amount to a caudillo in spite of the apparent or partial civilization of those countries, thus indicating that he possesses in a culminating degree the characteristic traits of his people, or the ability to balance and manage their various elements.

In countries where most of the men know their interests and are capable of exercising their rights, the government does not arise out of a need for it to be headed by an individual who is superior for his wisdom, ambition, or cunning, but out of the material impossibility that all humans can govern at the same time. Therefore those countries agree upon the best method of managing their affairs, and choose from among their ranks those whom they consider most capable of understanding and implementing that method, or propose ideas to them which they hold to be acceptable and useful.

A man is a robber if he receives for safekeeping a sum to be applied for the benefit of his employer and then administers it against his wishes or for his own benefit.

The vote is a more sensitive pledge than any other because, besides the interests of the voters, it is bound up with life, honor, and the future; and anyone who uses wrongly and against the voters the post which he owes to them, and in which he administers other people's affairs, is a robber.

The President's message is as simple and detailed as an end-of-the-year statement, lacking no firmness where needed to assure the administrated that their wealth is well protected, and not without those natural skills of an administrator content with his office, and who does his utmost to stay in it.

This inevitable enthusiasm which is awakened by leadership, even where it is more limited in power and brilliance, is united in Cleveland to the virtuous desire of seeing defeated, with his reelection to the Presidency, those who maliciously and willingly have ignored him and have distorted his honesty.

The message formulates anew a policy of practical wisdom,

foresight, and gradual change, which in Cleveland are connected.

In social questions, he sees that the sky is closing in and the clouds are piling up, hears the thunder and wants to stop the lightning.

In Treasury matters, which are at the root of the social restlessness, he wants industries to shed the excessive taxes that prevent them from producing goods at a low cost and accomodating the impatient, when not desperate, workers.

In politics, he knows that the country cares little about dogma, fears the creation of a cynical clique of self-appointed heads and holders of public office who distribute their wealth among themselves, and will keep the Democratic Party in power only if it appears able to govern impartially.

His message opens with an exposition of the state of international relations.

On that subject he foresees the need of restricting Chinese immigration at the same time as protecting the Chinese who are in this country; he warmly alludes to the Statue of Liberty, which confirms France's affection; he intimates that the Canadian fishing indutry's dispute might bring disagreeable consequences, for this industry is defended by the English government beyond its legitimate rights. He praises the importance of renewing the treaty with the Sandwich Islands,[4] in order not to lose to another nation this Pacific stronghold which has become an American trading post. He does not consider it wrong that, without any protection, the small republic of Liberia[5] be given a ship which is not much needed in the United States; he advocates greatest care in electing and maintaining the consular corps whose men must be intelligent and numerous. He favors an extension of the postal service, and an improvement in the mail service that now cuts across the River Platte, although it should not be in the form of concessions or subsidies. He recognizes the United

---

4. Sandwich Islands was the original name for Hawaii.

5. Liberia, a Negro Republic in Africa, was established by the American Colonization Society in 1822 with the aim of transporting free Blacks from the United States to it. Its independence was officially proclaimed in 1847, but the United States did not recognize it until the Civil War.

States' exceptional interest in Cuba,[6] and believes possible a friendly arrangement with Spain—one which would assure the North Americans of the advantages which he deems natural. And, resuming with discreet and necessary modesty the latest censurable controversy between the United States and Mexico, he seeks without much luck some means of gracefully withdrawing from that serious difficulty, emphatically affirming that—whilst it is most desirable that the reciprocity treaty put through in 1883 be implemented, "since Nature has made us irrevocable neighbors, and prudence and benevolence should make us friends,"—the United States must protest, and has protested, the Mexican law which authorizes that country's law courts to apply its penal code within said country to foreign subjects who, although they are outside of it and in the land of their own citizenship, might have committed against Mexican subjects crimes punishable under Mexican law.

And in the section of his message devoted to international affairs, he includes several recommendations, such as those that revise and establish laws of naturalization and extradition, to avoid disputes with friendly countries. He recommends that the high duties on foreign works of art be lifted, and copyright treaties be respected in sympathy with the Bern Convention accords.

Wise pages written in a solid and impregnable style appear in nearly all sections of the message dealing with the science of economy; or with the Treasury surplus which must be reduced to the level of necessary government expenses, "because an opportune concession usually avoids a violent and unwise action sometimes stemming from a delay in the application of justice"; with the workers' interests which among other things require a lowering of the tariff, "so that living costs may be reduced without reducing opportunities for work, or the worthy position that work holds in our estimation"; with the need to stop the minting of silver coinage, "because there is no longer any vault large enough in which to store the great quantity of minted silver, worth less than its face value, and which has no outlet into circulation." The message treats the justice of administering the Indian tribes more kindly and efficiently, since they are now peaceful, educable, and

6. President Grover Cleveland did not support the independence movement of Cubans, but rather favored Spanish domination of Cuba.

hard-working, "because the government cannot be freed of its responsibility until it civilizes the Indians, and enables them to care for themselves with their rights undisturbed." It deals with the duty of putting an end to the accumulation of land into greedy hands which acquire it wrongfully and fail to make it produce, nor do its owners reside upon it, "because it is not right to arouse just desires in the needy by that hoarding of useless or oppresive riches in the hands of avaricious companies, and in many cases in the hands of foreigners." The message includes the pension that must be paid to all disabled veterans, "because demanding it is not a right of this or that soldier's friend, but a national feeling, for the nation knows that it must, in their old age or poverty, attend to those who defended it with their lives." It deals with the urgency of addressing the differences between labor and capital "with a truly American sentiment which does not permit other men to be seen as servants, but as equals, and demands that all in the Republic cooperate toward its happiness and tranquility, and that capital respect and remunerate labor as it would a glorious brother in whose happiness lies its greatest security."

That describes every one of the message's ample and judicious sentences.

They are comfortable, bold, well distributed, and the thoughts move along them majestically.

The statesman's cloak hides the politician's mace.

The document is not lacking in arrogant contempt, as much trouncing, and some triumphant marches over the heads of his perverse adversaries.

Furthermore, every matter is treated so that, neither accusing nor defending the hostile Democrats, it plainly shows their injustice at the same time as it "takes the wind out of the sails" of the Georgists and Republicans, and he takes the place of the latter in the reforms which they loudly proclaim as their own, and meets the former halfway, acknowledging in their demands everything that is reasonable.

Because in politics one must be like Cleveland in this message: an elephant and a fly at the same time.

The message has now been read.

The press cannot find his Achilles' heel.

The country gives it unreserved praise. The very ones who noted a certain rudeness and harshness in Cleveland, understand that the harshness could have been prudence and the rudeness indignation.

The river is in sight, and the Democrats have to make a drastic decision.

They came to power to govern with the message's spirit if not with the precise laws recommended in it.

They are halfway through their administration. The experienced Republicans are lying in wait. The enthusiastic Georgists are moving forward.

If the Democrats—today divided into two hostile factions on the tariff question, and into two others on the question of public offices—do not energetically adjust their differences, lower taxes, stop putting their appetite for public offices above the need to moralize politics, or show some national stature in serious matters, either the parties are going to fall to pieces in time for the next Presidential election, or, in spite of their lamentable history, the Republicans will return to power because of their enemies' mistakes.

Parties are not kept in government unless their hands are free of interests, and their roots based in truth.

JOSÉ MARTÍ

La Nación, Buenos Aires, January 26, 1887

ELECTIONS!

THE PRESIDENTIAL CAMPAIGN IN THE UNITED STATES. — CAUSES, METHODS AND SIGNIFICANCE OF CLEVELAND'S DEFEAT. — CLEVELAND IN GOVERNMENT. — THE SITUATION FROM OUTSIDE AND WITHIN. — ELECTION DAY.

New York, November 2, 1888

To the Editor of *La Nación:*

The President has just been elected.[1] Some men are roaming over the city with their hats tipped back, their triumphant thumbs in the armholes of their vests, and the victory rooster, made of feathers or cardboard, hanging from their lapels. Others go about as if they were reluctant to be seen, with the defeated badge in their buttonholes, crestfallen and grim, paying the winners the money lost on their wagers. A flagpole without a flag upon the Democrats' buildings testifies to a sense of mourning; a vociferous flag, as if with new colors and luster, tells of the Republicans' victory as it furls and unfurls. West Virginia, counter to its opinions and history, finally yielding to the railroad interests, votes against the democracy, led by an enemy of the culpable practice of giving the railroads countless square miles of land and mountains of privileges. Delaware, where an irritated democracy rebels against the family that wishes to govern the State as if it were its fief,[2] goes Republican for the first time. The Democrat Cleveland is defeated in New York State where the local Democratic candidates win. Harrison, the advocate of protectionism, is victorious. And behind Harrison, letting the yellow glance of his ivory eyes fall upon his routed opponents, Blaine wins. Friends of the rich rise to power, and to the politics that continues to enrich them! Out of power the man who inaugurated a policy to calm the angry poor without threatening righteous wealth, or chastising unjust wealth immoderately!

<hr>

1. Benjamin Harrison was the Republican candidate for president, who ran against Grover Cleveland, nominee of the Democratic Party, who was seeking reelection. Harrison triumphed.

2. The reference is to the Dupont family, multimillionaires, who controlled the economic and political life of Delaware.

113

In the White House, around a table covered with forgotten tea and untouched food, when at dawn Cleveland—valiant Cleveland—discovered that his partisans' treason, as well as his enemies' bribery, denied him his reelection, the man suddenly fell silent, and his young wife kissed him upon with both cheeks, poorly restraining her tears. In the victor's house, whose wooden fence has been destroyed by the fanatic Republicans to keep the splinters as relics, the elected general—"Grandpa Benjamin"—and a little old white-haired lady with a shawl around her shoulders, appear arm in arm on the porch to receive the crowd's crazy congratulations. And after having seen the most beautiful act of freedom in both its greatness and its leprosy, after the campaign's noise and the silent voting, after the struggle of the factions and their magnificent resignation, after the solemn spectacle, the streets filled with sleepy drunks, the squares filled with frenetic heads, the hurrahs which a weary sun placed upon the wings of a beautiful night and which the night returned to the sun—after all of this the stranger in his rented house, when everything invites him to silence, is at a loss to be able to tell about it.

Let anyone come, even if the one who should have come has not. Over and above all the heroes' battles, the important thing is this peaceful exercise of the national will; what counts is the triumph of the people's spirit!

The horns and trumpets were still sounding yesterday, calling the citizens to vote from early in the morning; then there was a great silence, a painful silence as during a period of creation, and then a majesty as when one passes beneath porticos of light. After a year of vehement fighting, the two parties that stir up the emotions of twenty-five million men have changed their places in government. Eager party members have filled the cities to elbow, eulogizing together, making fun of the opposing candidates together, and the next day we see no more traces of the struggle—in the noise of the steamboats devouring their cargos, and of the bellowing railroad trains in the stations—than a few exhausted eyes and some wine-filled heads.

There were men who sold themselves for five dollars, and for two, and for a glass of whiskey; there was the imfamous traffic in ballots incited by the ever-dangerous coincidence between national,

State, and city elections. There was the fraud and bribery resulting from the poor manner of voting rather than from the voting institution itself; but man's human heart was gently moved when seeing one silk-hatted magnate and the stevedore in shirt and cap awaiting their turn in line before the glass and freshly cut pine ballot boxes, to harmoniously resolve the affairs of the nation. Watch over the worm; but never despair of the rose or curse it for attracting the worm with its beauty!

Cleveland is defeated, defeated by the interests of his opponents and the greed and perfidy of his own people.[3] For if he served his country rather than himself; if he endangered his certain election by putting before the country in time the truth that can avoid the enmity and clash of its elements; if he brought with him enough courage and kindness to establish the South in the government, to the anger of the ambitious and vengeful North—the South which might tire of being deprived of administering the Treasury to which it contributes, and of the laws from which it suffers, either because of passion or avarice; if he frightened away the party of the monopolies by his ability to organize a national campaign of resistance to the immoderate profits and freedom-destroying practices of the monopolizers; if he triumphed once by himself, against the advice and opposition of those party hypoorites who do not want any virile person with new ideas and superior strength for a standard-bearer, but rather a meek and timid weakling who shares real power with those who, in hopes of common profits, propose and extol nominal power; if in his own party he resisted the traffickers who see in politics a market of public offices, and those who, in payment for their support, demand unconscionable concessions to their vanities and hates, or to their misdemeanors and interests— then what fate was to befall him but that which, except in times of crisis, is the fate of virtue in politics? Virtue in politics is sucessful

3. Actually Cleveland received a greater popular vote than Harrison, but lost in the electoral college. The electoral college was established in Article II of the U. S. Constitution. Each state is entitled to a number of electors equal to its total representation in the House of Representatives and the Senate. The voters choose these electors who, on the first Monday after the second Wednesday in December following election day, meet at their respective state capitals and cast their ballots for President and Vice-President. Originally it was the plan to have the electors choose these individuals, but soon they simply voted for the candidates who won the presidential election by gaining a majority of the votes in the electoral college.

only tangentially, never directly and absolutely; its success does not lie in the conquest of power—almost always a reward for those who lower themselves to representing interest or emotion—but in exhibiting itself so constantly and wisely that the interested statesman that indicts and persecutes it dares not dispense with it entirely. Harassing him relentlessly, hanging upon his head, appearing at his banquets. Virtue is a whip rather than a bridle. It is useful when it lashes, and nearly impotent when it leads. Since all men are not yet virtuous, virtue cannot represent them naturally, unless to that lesser and governmental extent, the gift of a few politicians who are both honest and sagacious, which grants to greed and prejudice what it demands as a reward for refusing to oppose it.

Since he was the only Democrat whose novelty and personal power could remove from their scornful and monarchic chairs the Republicans who had been sitting in them for a quarter of a century, what efforts were the rich and overwhelmed Republicans not to make to overthrow the one who, by his bravery and unselfishness, showed the stature necessary to bring about the tariff reduction, as he had demonstrated by leading the debate on it, over and above both friends and enemies?

If the Republicans on the side of tax reform, like Cleveland, saw that its accomplishment by the Democrats would keep the rival party far from power for a long time, then how, with the petty logic of party interests, were they *not* to prefer to defeat the standard-bearer of their own victim, rather than see that victim succeed through the efforts of the opponents?

If all the monopolies, owned by prominent Republicans, have seen their privileges threatened during Cleveland's government, and if the favored industries have found him to be the patriotic adversary who brings about the nation's balance and well-being rather than the immoderate and detestable profits of a minority of industrialists, then how were the monopolies and protected industries *not* to dedicate their ill-gained surpluses to wrest from power anyone who shows a determination and capacity to oppose their being perpetuated in them?

116

If there are Democrats wrongly interested in keeping the high tariff under whose protection their privileged factories can sell at exorbitant prices—then how, by putting their personal interests above those of the Democrat who is threatening them, and above those of the country, will they *not* vote with their opponents who promise to support their privileges, rather than with the Democratic candidate who advises them to subordinate their surplus profits to public welfare and national peace?

If he refused to make public posts a feeding trough for hungry politicians, and to distribute public offices paid for by the entire nation as a recompense for services rendered to his party by hired speakers and vote traders—then why must the Democratic "associations," maintained for the conquest and common enjoyment of public posts, support a courageous President who wants to "win a reputation for purity by depriving of public offices those who have installed him in the Presidency?"

If with the fierceness of honesty he has disregarded the demands of New York's greedy minority whose treachery in the last elections put him at the point of losing the Presidency instead of being installed in it; if obeying its mandate he preferred to embody, in the party that owes him a return to national government, the ideas of reform which the restless country demands, rather than listen to the rancorous counsel of the New Yorkers who regard candidates to high position as only agents of the associated political power which exalts and maintains them for the associations' profits—then how were those New York Democratic associations that use popular ideas as a pretext, and renowned candidates as a disguise, to keep from preying upon him as they have done, and from blocking his path to power as they have done, on the pretext of aiding him? These associations place above all else the principle by which they exist, which is that of distributing positions among members of the associations which, with their disciplined army of voters, obtain the power needed to distribute those positions.

And if this time the election of a President who is hostile to the principle of piracy in politics coincided with the election of Governor Hill[4]—idol and head of the pirates—and with the election of the

---

4. David Bennett Hill (1843-1910), Democratic "boss" of upstate New York, was re-elected governor of the state.

city's mayor whom it will behoove, this coming year, to provide profitable positions—then how can they keep from "buying, knifing, kicking, and controlling," from giving their votes as Democrats to the Republican candidate (in opposition to the Democratic one whom they abhor for his virtue) in exchange for Republican votes ·for the Democratic governor who heads the associations, and for the mayor? Because the Republicans are more interested in winning the Presidency than in winning State governorship or the office of mayor.

Because Cleveland's tariff message, a basis of this election struggle, was opposed in vain by the Republican party whose important men and whose very own candidates to the White House and to the Vice-Presidency have been demanding for years, and have been putting before both halls of Congress, an even more energetic tariff reform bill than Cleveland's, and one already adopted by the House of Representatives. In vain has Blaine—who has already been named Prime Minister, in case of a Republican victory—slyly raised the cry of free trade, with false statistics, against a reform which scarcely touches the existing high tariff except to import vital articles and products at a lower cost, and remove import duties on those raw materials whose customs duty prevents Yankee industry from producing articles at prices to compete with those of the European factories. In vain did Blaine accuse Cleveland of treacherous leniency in defending the American fishing industry in Canadian waters because, basing himself upon the Republican Senate's refusal to approve the pending agreement with the English, Cleveland asked the senators for immediate authority, which they did not concede to him, to respond in reprisals, more energetically than anyone would have suggested, against the English government which Blaine accused of being Cleveland's accomplice because an occasional London journal upholding free trade praised his message the way that the North American newspapers were praising it.

In vain did the Republicans cunningly provoke the English minister in Washington to write, in response to one naturalized Englishman, a letter in which he encouraged him to vote for the Democrats, insinuating that they must not be regarded with annoyance because of the Canadian affair. Because when Blaine, in speeches smeared with curare, clutched the letter in his fist and waved it in the air as proof of Britannic interest in Cleveland's election, Cleveland waited in decorous calm (although as far as he was concerned the election was filled with danger during the last stages of the campaign) for England to reproach the intrusive minister, although perhaps less energetically than might be sufficient to disprove the rumor. And when British silence and the voice of the people authorized him to act independently, he sent his passport to the minister to the astonishment of the Republicans, the joy of the Irish, and unanimous praise from the nation before which Blaine straightway accused Cleveland of having sacrificed the minister to the desire of soliciting the lukerwarm vote of the naturalized Irish.

Prestige grew to such an extent that from Indiana itself—the State loyal to the Republicans where its Presidential candidate lived—news arrived that the Democrats might win the campaign. Most of the industries spoke out for reform. The standard-bearer for the lowering of customs duties was the owner of one of those marvellous foundries.

Business, instead of languishing or coming to a halt as in other elections, was confident and aggressive. Duty-free raw materials, and we shall have trado for our industries! Duty-free lumber, and we shall have ships for our commerce! Work for our textile mills and foundries, closed or half closed now, and we shall have peace among the workers! Duty-free wool, and we shall clothe the world! When a town of millionaires, bankers, stock brokers, industrialists, and importers passed in review before the President with these slogans upon their flags, in a driving rain one famous Saturday; when forty thousand businessmen in a row, cheering unceasingly, endured a rainfall which gave a larger greatness to that parade of free men, rich men, manufacturers, old men, consumptives, and cripples—the President's austere and energetic face, as he stood bareheaded to see them pass, certainly showed no signs of defeat!

The love of his wife and the people's esteem have forcefully and rapidly changed the harsh and ugly face of that man who was a bachelor governor three years ago, into this kindly and radiant face, and his heavy bovine body into this erect one. He was sure of his reelection—he who has felt the "knife thrusts" of his friends!

His joyful wife, wrapped in furs and caressing two children, watched him from the balcony of her hotel. And Blaine watched from an upper floor, alone.

But the Republicans' principal hope came from New York. Let us shake all this war hatred, and all the power of the railroads, all the influence of the favored industries, over the threatened or ignorant workers! But above all let us go to New York with all the money the monopolies may give! What matters, in case the election in the industrial and railroad worker States fails us, is to take New York's thirty-six electors away from Cleveland.

New York is the home of the wealthy who pay, and of the votes which are sold. New York is where Hill gives the orders, for he has the saloons on his side, and wants to take vengeance upon Cleveland who offends him with his honesty, and whose candidacy is blocking Hill's way to the Presidency. New York is the home of Tammany Hall, an association determined, at the cost of the Presidency which promises it no benefits, to take possession of the mayor's office, which must distribute such sinecures this time— sinecures of eighty thousand, fifty thousand, thirty thousand dollars a year. New York is the location of the County association headed by Hewitt, an able but vain old man who has lived with more prosperity than political courage, and who now, with some tardy and irregular fits, wants to be compared with Cleveland whom he abominates, even though he seems to be a Democrat like him, and may even permit his supporters to trade their vote with that of the Republican President to prevent Cleveland from winning, for he regards Cleveland as a fortunate rival, and so that he will not be defeated by the wealthy young man who, in order to advance politically, lends himself to be an invited guest of the other Democratic association, Tammany Hall, for mayor. In New York where the good President is hated, where the Democrats are fighting over the spoils, and where entire districts are for sale at five dollar a head!

Music, bonfires, nightly shouting, parades lasting for six hours— what is not bought by the enormous treasury of the monopolies! Is anything more required the day before election day? Let us go to Philadelphia, home of the protected industries. In a few hours,

120

when all the campaign expenses seem to be covered, an emissary raises half a million dollars. Is Indiana in danger? Well, there goes a cheque for three hundred thousand dollars to buy the undecided vote, which there—oh, how ignominious!—comes from this country's own men, from North American farmers!

What matter that the Reform Club, composed of some vigilant attorneys, may have denounced to a judge the hotels which the Republican fraternity is bribing with pure gold to leave blank entire pages of dates in arrears, and then fill them in with the names of people from who knows where—settlers who come from places where there are more than enough Republican votes, for the purpose of passing off as residents for a month past in places where they did not reside and have the right to vote? What matter that the Democratic merchants, assembled for purposes of permanent vigilance, may determine to have in each one of the 826 voting booths a sentinel who sees to it that the "associations" do not sell or change the vote, and an attorney to defend the Democrats whom the Republicans intimidate or accuse under false pretenses? All will be done, and the lion's flesh will be nibbled away bite by bite.

In a voting place where suffrage will be hostile to them, there will be witnesses installed to invalidate the vote so that, while one goes to the judge and returns, the ballot will reach the ballot box late, for the polls close at four o'clock.

In cases where a Democrat shows a desire to take revenge upon one of his fellow party members who defeated him in the candidacy, a thousand dollars is put under the table for him to put some free beer on the counter, and show his friends that the democracy would be better served this time by voting for the Republicans. And at the polling places where there is a string of workers' votes early in the morning—for they want to vote without losing a day's pay—the way will be found for the inspectors of the ballot boxes to appear after the clock strikes ten arm in arm with unknown friends and with rumpled banknotes showing in their vest pockets. In former years they were given new ones, the kind the banks give to businessmen; but now those crisp green ones recently come from the banknote engraver have been replaced by other rumpled and filthy ones which will not proclaim the bribery.

In the rest of the country the prestige of the protectionist system will be aided as much as possible, which is not little, although, aided by the protected factories' purses and by the workers' fear of losing their employment should they vote against their bosses, it will be even greater. But New York has three Presidential candidates: a Democrat, a Republican, and a Temperance one—plurality at all cost! What would the "leagues" of industrialists in the protected industries not give to bring to power the one who maintains that a rise in the price of necessities (thanks to the alliance of those who produce them aided by the tariff) does not suit the country which pays the tariff? What would they fail to give to throw from power anyone who—instead of supporting his candidacy with money accumulated by this continuing fraud to the nation, by the guaranteed collection of unfair prices, by the interests of the least, protected by the nation against the interests of the most—appears as a candidate against the defrauders? Let emotion or opinion cast ninety thousand votes; the lack of eleven thousand is bought with fifty-five thousand dollars!

That is why all members of the "leagues" of industrialists who stifle competition and impose forced prices upon their products are Republicans; and the usurers headed by Morton, the millionaire candidate to the Vice-Presidency; and the railroads which are gobbling up the finest lands of the new States, and have "Grandpa Benjamin," the Presidential candidate, as their favorite advocate in the Senate and law courts. The Senate now belongs to the railroads and millionaires. Much of the House of Representative belongs to them, whether because of an election paid for with their funds, or because of a partial purchase. Well, now to the Presidential chair with a famous Stock Market speculator for Vice-President, and for prime minister the one who—by recognizing that with a high tariff the industries cannot produce goods at prices to sell, or the workers have the work they demand—finds it natural and comfortable to impose his iniquitous prices upon others rather than reduce the profits of the wealthy minority who abuse their people in their own country and, under the cloak of Americanism and some international niceties, propose Spanish American congresses[5] under the wing of the White House as an occasion to arrange—by means of frivo-

5. The reference is to the forthcoming Pan-American Congress to be held in Washington. All the republics of Latin America, except Santo Domingo, sent delegates.

122

lous enthusiasm or intimidation—predatory commercial treaties that balance the confusion for the profit of the industrial oligarchy of the North, with prices imposed in the smallest countries of America upon Yankee products of obligatory purchase.

And the city never saw such a hard-fought struggle, for all through October it was like the dwelling of two armies in a truce. There were never more speeches, songs and their refrains, insignia and uniforms, scuffles with sticks and fists, parades costing a hundred thousand dollars with hundreds of bands and fifty thousand torches. There was never so much decorum in discussions because of the nobility with which Cleveland's message presented the electoral theme, nor a greater contrast between the repose of the Democrats, sure of winning, and the aggressive impetus of the Republicans, although the politeness of both was astounding as they peacefully crossed each other in the streets with their flags and their bands. Those with red flags went to the right, and those with the country's flag to the left. Only on the final nights did they come to blows when a cavalry of blue- and white-garbed Negroes charged the red-capped Democrats who were barring their way, not without most of them paying with their blood, since the tin axes suddenly functioned as weapons, and the petroleum of the torches burned more than one gilt helmet. This took place in front of the houses where the parties had their general headquarters, and which night after night were the meeting places of the opposing factions, until the mortifying refrains drove them crazy and they punched each other in the chins just as the ubiquitous police were using their nightsticks on the lawyers and students who formed a large part of the riot. Some of them treated their pommeled shoulders with cognac from Delmonico's[6] and others, between soda and absinthe, rested their bruised legs upon Hoffman's[7] easy chairs.

The last parade of the Republicans took six hours to pass by: the last parade of the Democrats was a river of fire by night, and its lights made it look like a Persian festival. All was fifes and drums and bugles. Down one street went the ship owners with a wooden ship drawn by eight richly caparisoned horses; down another went

6. Delmonico's was a famous restaurant in New York City.

7. James Thompson Hoffman (1828-1888), lawyer, politician, Mayor and Governor of New York City and State.

the tobacco growers with fans made of tobacco leaves. They ran into the cotton planters who had tufts of cotton on their lapels, and stopped to make way for the pottery shop workers who had tricolor porcelain cups in their buttonholes; down another street came the law students with clubs for walking sticks and brooms over their shoulders as a sign of victory. The carpenters brought a huge rooster upon a litter. Up the street one could hear the railroad trains, and down the street snatches of music and gusts of voices. All was flags, signs to attract the attention, and clamor. Man was prepared to exert himself, and on the pretext of political emotion he announced his kingly power with the handsome enthusiasm of a victorious camp. The hired parades passed by languidly, the participants with gleaming oilskin capes over their filthy Prince Alberts, and carrying flameless torches.

But after all the shouting, that was like an awning, election day dawned serenely clear and sublimely silent to all that grandstand of fire burning from river to river above the vibrant city. When it grew light the last of the bugles called the voters from under their windows. It is six o'clock; get up so that all the party's votes are in the ballot boxes before four! Every district has its captain, every neighborhood its lieutenants, every street its Republican guard who awakens those of his political party, and its Democratic guard who awakens his own. It is a holiday! But not for all the workers because they do not want to lose a day's pay. To prevent the enemy from keeping count, nobody wears his insignia any more. There are 826 polling places in the city. At one hundred feet from each of them, beside the pine election kiosks covered with placards and pictures of the candidates, are the ballot distributors of each candidacy, men for hire at five dollars a day, with treason in their eyes, and the ballots in a white bag. In the morning when the sun came out, they still did not dare to sell the interests which they were paid to keep!

Two black-helmeted policemen, nightsticks in hand, stand guard at the polling place door. The polling place is a barber shop, a tobacco store, a flower shop, or a stationer, rented for such use by the municipality, and while the folded paper ballots are dropped into the ballot boxes, and after the inspectors check the voter's residence and name, and while one secretary from each party writes them down, another policeman with a nightstick upon his knees reads his newspaper seated like a king upon a shoeshine boy's chair, and in the rear of the stores beards are trimmed, newspapers sold, and flowers tied in bunches. The silent single file row of people stretches from the door round the block.

The sun shines and the children wander about. A toothless Irishman holds out his bundle of ballots in front of Tammany Hall's kiosk. The man at the Republican kiosk spies upon the well-dressed. The County man rushes upon the approaching voter to prevent his Tammany rival from speaking to him first. Each party's watchman, with a fine hat and a stylish overcoat, goes from one to another in the waiting line, whispering. Oh, what a line! A merchant of gigantic bearing stands a head above the rest; he wears a top hat and has a serious expression. A shirtless wretch with bloodshot eyes and a short coat buttoned up to his chin stands behind him, a bundle of ballots in his trembling hand; he is followed by a dandy in an English suit, a bowler hat perched on the back of his head and patent leather boots; a strong-fisted working lad with a healthy face stands tall above him; an Italian with hair cut in the Capoul fashion and a twisted mustache boasts a small gray beaver hat and a false stickpin in his necktie. What is an Italian doing here? "How are you, Michael old chap?" a policoman asks the shirtless wretch who responds that he is all right, and introduces him, with the airs of a gentleman, to an old man with a picaresque cleanshaven face who shows off his silver walking stick in front of him. Who can that be for everyone to draw aside for his arrival? An invalid in a wheelchair coming to vote with his two sons.

And in the polling places of the heavily populated districts the voting was so diligent that by ten o'clock mountains of white appeared through the glass of the ballot boxes. In other polling places some Neapolitans with their pipes and hats, their sack coats and earrings, came in—in flocks led by their boss, to vote upon the affairs of a country whose language they fail to speak, at a dollar an ear. They look like Merino sheep with dirty fleece, and like muddy worms! Why does that Irishman come to cast a vote for which he is given a gallon of whiskey which he leaves hidden in an entryway next door? You illiterate Russian Jew, why for a new jacket or a dollar do you come to influence, by voting for a name that means nothing to you, the public affairs of which all you know is the profit you receive from selling them out? You bearded irate German, what right do you have to exercise the freedom you despise? You rachitic gipsy, why do you gnaw Washington's silken waistcoat? You Foreigner, why with your mercenary feelings do you unsettle the nation that gave you asylum?

"Here, here!" to the County kiosk where they are selling the Democratic Presidential candidacy to elect Democratic Hewitt to the mayoralty! Here, to old man Hewitt! Two Democratic votes for Harrison for one mayoral vote for the old man! To Tammany, to the Tammany kiosk where one Democratic vote for Harrison is offered in exchange for one Republican vote for Hill! We are "knifing" the President! And what has this President Cleveland done for "the boys?" "In the soup, in the soup!" cry some young boys as they pass by, adopting this election refrain for their own. Cleveland is falling "into the soup!" pushed by the party members who prefer the virtuous President's defeat to the defeat of Hill, the governor who distributes contracts and employment among "the boys," and to the loss of the governor's office which this year is disposing of public posts which will produce about eighty million dollars in the period. Let the leader fall behind, and him who lets himself be led move ahead! All votes for Harrison, all the votes he needs to be elected, provided that the eighty million remains in our hands, in the hands of Tammany.

We took revenge on this conceited person, we kept the State and the cities! Three votes for Harrison here for one for Grant, head of Tammany! More votes for Harrison in exchange for votes for Hewitt, head of the County! One vote for Harrison for one for Coogan, head of the Labor Party of Father McGlynn,[8] who has sunk from evangelist to politician! Here, to the kiosks of the Democrats, one vote for Harrison! In vain do the votes of the independent Re-

8. At the beginning of the campaign to elect Henry George Mayor of New York on the United Labor Party ticket in 1886, many, if not a majority, of the Catholic priests supported George. But as the campaign advanced, "at the suggestion" of the "higher Catholic powers" all Catholic priests except Father Edward McGlynn (1837-1900) withdrew from active participation on behalf of the Labor Party candidate and single-tax advocate. On September 29, 1886, Archbishop Michael Augustine Corrigan (1839-1902), a strong conservative, forbade Father McGlynn to speak at a scheduled public meeting on behalf of George. Father McGlynn disobeyed, and was suspended from exercise of his priestly functions for a period of two weeks.

publicans, and of the people with free ideas who vote wherever they see some reason, oppose the sold suffrage of the Democrats. "Four, four, four more years!" the frantic young boys sing to the beat of a drum as they go by. "Four, four, four more months!" repeat both Republicans and Democrats, arm in arm and laughing, before the kiosks.

And in a poor district filled with Italians and Irishmen, the hunting has no limits. The people manning the kiosks prop up a half-drunk voter in the darkness of a vestibule. "Thanks to Hill," says a kiosk keeper, "this year we haven't been given the ballot reform law ordering a voter to write his vote secretly inside the voting booth!'"'Tom, a dollar if you vote for that good Democrat, fat man Campbell, who is as drunk as you are! Two dollars, Tom, two dollars if you vote for the Republican MacCarthy, who will spring you from jail when you fall down dead from whiskey! Here goes Pete who wants five dollars!"

"In the entryway, Pete, where the police can't see you! There they are, looking for Campbell, looking for Irishmen! Step aside, you rogues, I'm voting for Harrison because I fought with him in the war! Who dares to insult me? I'm a textile worker who's been out of work for six months, and I pay a dollar for poor quality American-made cloth worth ten cents, so I'll vote for Cleveland! Here comes Tim Campbell with his vest unbuttoned, jewelry hanging down to his belly, a solitaire on his shirt bosom, with an ashen face and bloodshot eyes, flanked by two freckled characters hiccoughing and laughing: 'Let's have a drink, cops, let's have a drink, boys!'"

At last it is four o'clock! Begin the count in the closed polling places. Open the front doors of the saloons—the side doors have been open all the time. Swallow your impatience, you loyal party members, you honest voters. To the gutter, you have had quite

---

enough to drink and have gone on a spree with your election pay. To the cellar, you Neapolitans, to stash away the year's two dollars in your boots. Party associations, go to receive the news. Hotels, get ready for the nights' crowds. Have some weak tea, you nervous candidates.

And up the street a procession of young boys, each one with a board over his shoulder, taken from the wooden kiosks. The rival bands argue tooth and nail over those pine boards. A captain leads the procession with a placard of Coogan for a work apron, and an American flag for a sword; his lieutenant carries a placard of Hewitt, tied around his waist with a cord, like a skirt; two Rinconetes[9] go behind, their faces covered with phlegm and dirty arms around each other's shoulders, one six years old and the other about four. The six year old's coat drags on the ground, and both are barefoot. Then comes an empty barrel upon a platform, serving as a drum. Four people carry away the kiosk's four walls which came off whole, serving as large shields. Those with shaved heads go behind them at a military gait, some of them buxom and handsome, others mangy and gruff. The older ones in jackets, ugly and with, cruel faces carry stones as they bring up the rear.

By six o'clock the wave began to grow, and by midnight the squares were like oceans of heads, the hotels living masses, the gatherings of the defeated like tombs. Tammany Hall, the victorious association, was in a frenzy, and the air in front of the besieged newspaper buildings was filled with shouting, blowing horns, and trumpets. At each announcement, anger and cheers. Cleveland is winning, for in spite of the treason he is carrying the city, and nobody wants to see the caricatures which the rival magic lanterns have thrown upon their announcement banners to entertain the public. A young woman lets go of her companion's arm and gives him a kiss. A well-dressed man hails the news with outspread arms, his face filled with the agony of happiness. A noble-browed octo-

9. This may be a reference to "Rinconete," one of the characters in Miguel de Cervantes' *Rinconete y Cortadillo*, one of the picaresque stories in his *Novelas exemplares* (1613). The two boys depicted in the article partly resemble Rinconete's description.

genarian removes his hat, unafraid of the night air, and the lady friend with him, a woman with curly white hair and a silk hairnet, cheers the election returns by waving her bandana. The *Tribune*[10] building, the newspaper of Blaine who is supporting the apparently defeated Harrison, remains empty beside the *Sun,* which gave the first news. Patrols of hoarse young boys are marching to the sound of drums upon the sidewalk, the only unobstructed path. Above the uproar rise the cries of the newsboys, like a colossal flock of birds. One suddenly turns around and sees a field of bandanas, and it looks like the waves of a red sea. But the decisive news soon arrives: a Democrat who has lost his bet appears dressed like a tiger to walk around all the city's telegraph poles. Thousands of dollars change hands in smoke-filled hotel rooms; and when the *Tribune* banner announced the Republican victory, the crowds started moving all together, pushing rudely, leaving the Democrat alone, and with church-like unction intoned a hymn of triumph before the victorious newspaper. "Let's go!" said the angry octogenarian to his lady friend with the curly white hair.

JOSÉ MARTÍ

10. The New York *Tribune,* edited by Whitelaw Reid (1837-1912), was the leading Republican paper in the country.

INAUGURATION

THE ARRIVAL AND DEPARTURE OF A PRESIDENT IN THE UNITED STATES. — FESTIVITIES AND CEREMONIES. — POPULAR FESTIVITIES, OFFICIAL AND SOCIAL FUNCTIONS. — CLEVELAND. — HARRISON.

To the Editor of *La Nación:*

"Come, Mr. Secretary, give me your umbrella, because this one isn't big enough for two Presidents; you'll see that it will be returned, for we who ride in this carriage are honest people." The sorrel horses start off, the Negro coachman puts the whip in its holder, and from an energetic start the carriage arrives at the Capitol in a driving rain. Harrison steps out first, and then Cleveland.

That is how the United States changes its government. Here we look upon the enormous crowds soaked to the bones, hat brims pulled down to the shoulders, for it has been raining for six days. We are witnessing the night before the notable day, an inhuman night because of the inclemency of the weather and of men; the courtesies, customs, and ceremonies of the Presidential inauguration when one President takes leave of office and another enters it; the policies of the new one who wants industries protected, steamers subsidized, restraints upon immigration, and more continental power. We are considering a White House saddened to have its pretty mistress leave; a grandiose and ridiculous parade with its heroes and clowns; and a ball in a salon of columns so large that four men cannot encircle one of them with their outstreched arms; a White House where, at five dollars a head, both Negroes and white people stroll together beneath the flag-bedecked ceiling, eager to see the new President's wife in her apricot silk dress.

Who talks about Samoa, or the naturalized German taking sides in Congress and the press with their adoptive land against the land of their birth? Who discusses the conference on the struggles between the Americans and Germans on the island? What conversation is there about the half million dollars voted by the House for its station upon Samoa? Who is engaged in censuring or praising the endorsement of the Nicaraguan Canal project[1] which has been a singular procedure on the very days when Senator Edmunds asks for an official declaration of the displeasure with which the United States government would view France's endorsement of the Panama Canal project?[2] Who even ponders the already public plan to purchase Cuba,[3] where the blood that has not yet dried was shed in the name of the same charter of principles that made its neighbor rebel against its masters, without that astute neighbor extending a single bandage, without extending its arms?[4] Who is thinking about Lincoln's annual memorial service which was yesterday, or Washington's which was celebrated by theatrical performances and parades, or the four new States which used to be a palace of bisons and a virgin prairie with a fallow deer buck as lord, when half a century ago four thousand Federalists came to see President Harrison's grandfather take office carrying his gold-handled cane?[5] And today it is the Dakotas, North and South, Montana, Washington State[6] with its cathedrals made of the petrified wood of its forests, and the rich and avid nation that sent thousands of its citizens, with sprays of wheat in their buttonholes, to march in the fifty thousand man parade with which that nation—home of forty-two free nations—is

1. The project was the effort of the Maritime Canal Company of Nicaragua to build a canal through Nicaragua.

2. A French canal company, headed by Ferdinand de Lesseps, to dig a waterway through Panama, had gone bankrupt. But a new Panama Canal company had acquired its assets as well as an extension of its canal rights from Colombia until 1904.

3. Several plans by the United States to purchase Cuba from Spain had been made before, but all had failed.

4. Martí is referring to the shameful role played by the United States government during Cuba's Ten Years' War for independence (1868-1878). Not only did the United States give no help to the Cuban independence fighters, but openly supported Spain throughout the conflict. [For a detailed discussion of this role, *see* Philip S. Foner, *History of Cuba and its Relations with the United States*, Vol. II, 1845-1895 (New York, 1965), Chapters 17, 18, 20.]

5. Martí is referring to William Henry Harrison, the grandfather of Benjamin Harrison, who was elected President of the United States in 1848. He died in office shortly after being inaugurated.

6. Washington was admitted as the 42nd state on November 11, 1889. Montana was admitted as the 41st state on November 8, 1889. The state of South Dakota was admitted on November 2, 1889 as the 39th state and North Dakota as the 40th state.

134

celebrating the rise to power of Harrison's grandson, in his twill frock coat and double-soled shoes.

Two hundred thousand people have arrived in Washington for the inauguration ceremonies. Tomorrow, the gossip of Blaine and his rivals; the problems of the South with its Negroes determined to live; the revision of the demand of New Mexico which also wants to be a State instead of a territory, although there is scarcely anyone there who can read the language in which its laws are to be framed.[7] The trains are arriving, a flag at every window, their loads of Californians coming from the Pacific in their plush hats; with people of the Sioux tribe bringing carts sheathed in corn husks; with Texan cowboys wearing leather jackets, fringed trousers buttoned down both sides, overblouses, and Mexican sombreros; with Arkansas hunters in cotton coats and a deer's tail on their hats. Where will this throng of fanatics, pugilists, politicians, office seekers, the curious, peddlers, vagabonds, and robbers find lodgings? Upon chairs because there are no beds, upon rickety tables placed over bathtubs, resting their elbows on store counters, sleeping over their whiskey or milk, visiting brothels where the girls on display wear the dresses they put on for the first time when a new President is inaugurated; or walking on and upon the sticky asphalt in mud up to their ankles—water in their hearts, valises swollen with collars and cuffs, their petitions torn to pieces.

A loaf of bread costs a dollar; a seat in the kitchen, five. "I'm sharing my room," says a hunch-back actor, "with twenty-two intimate friends."

In the next room is Prince Harry, son of the journalist New, and the chicken salad he eats and the champagne he drinks with his dear old friends whose hats are pulled down in back! And Armour,[8] the great Chicago meat packer who has a whole floor in a hotel for himself alone, that costs him a mine a day! There outside past packs of Negroes huddled in a doorway, a procession of the wretched goes by, dragging their useless umbrellas. One of them sleeps leaning

----

7. New Mexico, one of the areas seized from Mexico after the Mexican War (1846-1848), had largely a Spanish-speaking population.

8. Philip Armour (1832-1901), industrialist and organizer of Armour & Company, meat packers.

against a pedestal, changing positions with every change of wind. Another, under cover of night, cowers against the legs of a statue of a horse.

But the White House has not turned off its lights. On its upper floors the women are awake, unable to sleep! His faithful secretary at a desk nearby, the hard-working President is in his office studying the laws that await his signature, approving them or rationalizing his veto[9] as if he had not heard the insulting songs of the crowds outside. He takes off his spectacles, rubs his eyes, and replaces those spectacles again.

The early morning is cold, and the logs upon the hearth seem to be talking and saying goodby. "I approve with all my heart of giving Sheridan's widow a pension." "What they want with this bill to return the taxes directly to the States, is to have the surplus disappear artificially, when what is necessary is to have its source disappear—the excess of import rights which leave us without any foreign trade, and with social uprising at the door. I'll veto that tax return bill even if I'm eaten up alive by criticisms!" The outcries increase: "In the soup, in the soup!" shout the groups standing at the windows: "Goodby, Grover, sweet Grover!" And we can hear outbursts of laughter, grunting, and whistling! There is dancing in the portico. People start knocking upon the windows. The President removes his spectacles, lays them upon a piece of paper which crackles as if something were shaking it, and raises his head. "Sir, Sir," says his secretary, rising from his chair and consoling him for his hurt. "Never mind, friend Lamont, never mind! if these men can insult me like that, I can bear it!" And he replaces his spectacles.

"I'm vetoing this bill that grants ten thousand dollars from the national Treasury to build a bridge where nobody even knows if there's a river." "I'm vetoing this unfair pension to a great-uncle of a soldier who never even fought in our battles." At four in the morning he rises from his desk: "See you soon, Lamont; I'll be here at eight."

9. A presidential veto could only be overridden by a two-thirds vote of both houses of Congress, the House and the Senate.

And at eight Washington was like a living mass. The streets had been filling since dawn; the vendors selling sausages and coffee were hawking their wares; an aide-de-camp passed by in great haste, his feathered hat wrapped in a handkerchief; curious women showed their faces from between drawn curtains. In their night-shirts and sleeping caps magnates went to the windows to see the red-jacketed firemen pass by; New York's Seventh Regiment in their pearl-gray uniforms; the Maryland delegation with monkey, bear and 'coon skins covering their chests like cuirasses; Republicans from Indianapolis, Harrison's city, with their tricolored umbrellas; people from Omaha behind a gigantic broom of green esparto grass with a red and blue handle. One cannot cross the broad avenue because two wires have been strung along the sidewalks to keep the crowds from darting into the parade. But the masses of people, water streaming down their necks, invade the steps on the avenue, wander about the empty grandstands, seek shelter from the freez-ing wind beneath gleaming umbrellas that shine like seashells in the heavy fog where the buildings cast shadows as enormous and confused as monsters. Bursts of music explode in the air, clashing and vanishing.

"Maryland, my Maryland!" play the fifes. "Marching through Georgia!" plays a drum and bugle corps leading the war cripples; a blue-jacketed and black-hatted band plays "America." "Here, here, buy these sausages from me, for on a day like this everything sells." "Who'll buy these dollar-size distaffs from me—they're like the one Martha Washington[10] had in her room for spinning!" "For one silver coin the man, the man himself with his projecting forehead and the beard reaching to his chest, on this sterling silver-handled cane!" As much pie as you can eat for just ten cents!" "Oh, it's only eight o'clock!" says a poor blind man who falls down exhausted; "Don't take me away, don't touch me; I want to die here, but I must see President Harrison first!"

"Three cheers for Cleveland!" cries a broad-shouldered man a head taller than that Republican crowd. "We're going to charge him dearly for those cheers!" says a birdlike man, peering out from beneath his neighbor's sleeve; "Well then, come and charge me for them!" "This fellow here is Beaver, General Beaver, with one leg

10. Martha Dandridge Washington (1732-1802), wife of George Washington.

less!" "Here comes a coachman arrested for charging a lady twenty dollars for a ride."

"Yes, Harrison visited Cleveland yesterday, and he was received very well; they talked about the weather." "And Cleveland paid a visit to Harrison, at four o'clock." "What did they talk about...?" "The weather!"

And so the sidewalks are swelling with people, the grandstands filling up, the soldiers entering in rows, the photographers taking group pictures, the agile Negroes shepherding the rich foreigners back and forth—or having their noses tweaked, or strewing witticisms about. Friends gather in cliques, with badges upon their breasts—the northerners stout, the southerners lean, the campaign actresses in rubber raincoats and hoods.

A prize fighter, smelling of violets, goes by with a cigar hanging out of his mouth, on the arm of one of New York's elegant gentlemen in a pilgrim's cloak and serge trousers. A leading citizen of Philadelphia, who gave ten thousand dollars to the election, rides by in a carriage, and he now has one office seeker on his trail for every dollar. General Tracy, a wealthy lawyer from Brooklyn and the new Secretary of the Navy, goes by with joy in his eyes, shaking hands and smiling. Others, the disconsolate candidates, go by in a gloomy mood, one of them as if he had just stopped crying into his long white beard like an afflicted child. Still others, drunk on wine, are joyful and vigorous because "These fellows—God damn the Democrats—these fellows are going to give us subsidies for the steamers! To Joe Chambertin, boys, to good champagne!" Some tardy militiamen, **their** heels at their waists, their guns like bludgeons, are running with their rain capes flying in the wind.

A father with a child upon each shoulder talks with a veteran seated upon the base of a street lamp, and tells him he is acquainted with Harrison. The other one claims to know him better, for he "fought with the President." That his son, the one upon his right shoulder, is taller than Harrison: "it's on horseback that you see men!" That Harrison chews tobacco, "Virginia tobacco!" That Harrison is afraid of dying in the White House.

"Like his grandfather, poor old man, who couldn't show off his plush hat for more than six weeks!"[11] This morning three crows flew cawing out of the Hotel Arlington where Harrison is staying: "That is what whiskey is for, to keep him alive!" And chased by the "rookie" police, the Pennsylvania volunteers push people out of the way, with blood in their eyes and falling down drunk, cursing and striking out with the butts of their guns. One of them gathers some rain in his shako, and wants to give a drink to a farmer carrying a cotton umbrella. Another turns his face to the sky and opens his mouth wide, because he is "very thirsty." The avenue cheers and we hear the bugles and cavalry; furious rain beats down upon the drums. A gentleman in natty attire jumps out of his coupé and enters Arlington Hotel with three bunches of roses.

"Hurray!" "Hurrah!" A hundred umbrellas suddenly open. Here come the daughters of the man who is going to be President. Here come their husbands with the little one in arms—the famous "government babies." Here comes the President's wife, her eyes sparkling, holding a bunch of flowers. "Hurrah again!" "God guide you, General!" "God bless my dear little general!" cries an elderly Negro woman who suddenly appears from amid the tricornes and cutlasses, her chin upon her knees. Here comes Benjamin Harrison, pale and unsmiling, his face showing anxicty, his legs short, heavy, above the waist. "To Willard!"[12] to meet President Cleveland so they can go to the Capitol together. There was a mistake in the rendezvous plans, and Harrison lunched too early—lunched standing, because "I can't sit down!" No, he will not await, even if it is not the time; on to the White House!

In the White House they were not expecting the visit so soon, even if the Blue Room was already fragrant with flowers, filled with palms and ferns, and even if the crystal chandeliers were brilliantly lit. The servants went silently back and forth; Cleveland's wife, already dressed for her departure, was seated closer to her mother than ever, in her dismantled room. Trunks and hampers were being taken out by the back door; from one of the hampers fell a copy of the Constitution, worn from use; a Negro page gives the

11. This is a reference to the fact that William Henry Harrison **died** only after six weeks in office.

12. A leading hotel in Washington, D.C.

coachman a vase of lilies and tells him to handle it carefully. Before a full-length portrait of Harrison's grandfather, Cleveland was signing the last of the proposed laws with his studious hand. "Are they here already? I'm coming right away." He rose slowly, his hands upon the portofolio that has seen so much work, buttoned his frock coat securely over his chest, and bid farewell to the servants who entered in a rush. It was a long, friendly, affectionate farewell: "One can very well make a President wait to say goodby to a good servant!" On to the Capitol in that open landau! The rain beats against them for a greeting, and they laugh as they enter the carriage filled with beaver coats—Harrison first. Of the two senators with them, one wants to open his umbrella and breaks one of its ribs. "An umbrella, Mr. Secretary!" All hats are tipped at the same time, because in a window, resting upon her mother's shoulder, is Cleveland's wife, bidding him farewell with a smile. She returns to the window with her hat on when the carriage is far away, and when her carriage leaves the portico, a wagonload of gifts arrives, the driver asking for the new President's grandchildren.

Scarcely a whisper, like a soft buzzing of bees, is heard in the hall filled with senators where a way is kept clear solely for the approaching Presidents; red faces and bald heads stand out from that dark mass of people. In a seat of honor Ingalls,[13] the slanderer with a forest of white hair, his round eyes behind spectacles, fans his calm face with a palm leaf fan. To the right are the black-robed magistrates of the Supreme Court and their martial chief justice, the poet Fuller. To the left are the foreign ministers—the minister from Germany with so much gold on his uniform that the cloth and his retinue with their cuirasses and plumage are not noticed; the minister from Siam in his brightly colored robe and pointed hat; the Chinese in yellow with his buttonned skullcap worn for important ceremonies; the Turk in his fez; the Japanese in his dress coat.

Whom are they applauding? Hannibal Hamlin,[14] Vice-President under Lincoln, as he enters with the step of a young man, wearing

13. John James Ingalls (1833-1900), Republican leader and U.S. Senator from Kansas (1873-1891).

14. Hannibal Hamlin (1809-1891), Maine abolitionist, elected vice-president of the United States with Abraham Lincoln in 1860; U.S. Senator from Maine (1848-1857, 1869-1891).

a wide silk cravat and squared-off coattails. And now? Blaine, a target for all eyes, upon whom some people rush, and others—senators Edmunds and Sherman—turn their backs. And now who is it? The main doorman entering with a pointer to set back the hands of the clock, because the law demands that the swearing-in ceremony take place at twelve, therefore he must set back the clock so the ceremony will be held on time.

Applause comes from the galleries which are filled with representatives who have had to fight hard to force their way in the sister House, and with the senators' wives and lady friends. There is Harrison's wife in a black and gold hat and a dark green suit; his daughter in green and white with a shining bonnet; his daughter-in-law in cardinal red trimmed with Russian fur; the wife of the Vice-President elect, with her five daughters, wearing pale green and silver. There is Blaine with his wife and favorite son who will be his secretary. Ingalls' sons who are very close to their father; and who read and make sensible selection for him, which is most helpful for a man that has to engage in debates.

No noted beauty or political lady was missing in the gallery. "Why didn't Cleveland's wife come?" "Well, I know that she herself was preparing a luncheon for Harrison's people this morning!" "Oh, what furs, what magnificent furs Morton's wife is wearing!" "That woman's hat could not have cost less than a hundred dollars!" "The German minister is really handsome!"

The gavel sounds, and men and women rise to their feet, for Cleveland is entering on the arm of a senator, amid loud applause; the Democrats find him healthy, the Republicans sickly.

The gavel pounds again to receive the President-elect, the people standing; when he arrives on the arm of Senator Hoar,[15] applause breaks out; his face is pale but his step is firm; he is short, well-known for his short size, but he seems tall for the occasion, and because stature is largely in the eye of the beholder. His nose caves in toward the space between his eyebrows from which rises his high and globular forehead shaped like a pear; he is tight-lipped and

15. George Frisbie Hoar (1826-1904), U.S. Senator from Massachusetts (1877-1904), Civil Service reformer and anti-imperialist.

has cold pale eyes; his beard is long and sparse. He sits beside Cleveland who makes him laugh with what he says; he looks about for his wife and children, and his eyes become calm as soon as he sees them.

At the third blow of the gavel Levi Morton,[16] the banker Vice-President, comes in with another senator. Morton is accustomed to walking upon carpets, is well combed and clean shaven, has smiling eyes and thin lips, and goes to a seat of honor as if he owned it. He swears what the resilient Ingalls, who thanks the Senate, from which he received compliments yesterday for his fine manner of presiding, asks him to swear with his oratorial voice. Ingalls declares the fiftieth Congress at an end, and hands the gavel to the Vice-President. With the brief and poorly constructed phrases of a man who is used to paying for them, Morton greets the extraordinary session—convoked for a change in power—and calls it to order. The people in attendance glance toward the door, seeking an exit. The people in the gallery put on their overcoats as they do during the final scene of a play. The new senators take their oaths of office four at a time, with the exception of one Quaker who merely promises. The time has come, the time for the new President to swear to the people—the crowds of people, the people closing in around the Capitol as if they were going to lift it up by the roots—that he will use for their benefit the authority he receives from them. The entire Senate, the robed justices, the multi-colored diplomats, and the illustrious ladies proceed to the deserted platform in the rain that is falling unmercifully. And when a cannon blast announces him, when the crowds see their hero appear, one could believe that the rain had ceased, because the tremendous cheering was like a canopy that grew in waves as if a flock of eagles were spreading over the city. The great cheering comes to an end, and at every movement of the man who is to be President—when he converses for an instant with the eighty-year old patriarch Hamlin, when he gestures refusal to an eager admirer who offers him a muffler, when he approaches the Chief Justice who hands him a Bible upon which he will swear to govern by God and the nation, when he kisses the Bible with the timid kiss of a fervent Protestant —there bursts from under that "sea of umbrellas" round after

16.   Levi Parsons Morton (1824-1920), New York banker, vice-president of the United States under Benjamin Harrison (1889-1893).

round of applause, like gunshot, from "the people outside who are unable to lose their cheerfulness." The flags droop miserably and cling to the columns because of the rain; the banners have turned into streamers licking their flagpoles; the senators appear by way of the portico, their coat collars turned up to their eyebrows, and do not dare to approach the Presidential group like Harrison's wife or Morton's wife who trip gayly along as if the rain were sunshine. The chairs are wells and almost everyone is standing, the justices in their robes and hooded cloaks, a Japanese man poking with the feather of his dress hat the neck of an irate general who counterattacks with his tricorne; ladies who want to hear better; Morton's eldest daughter, her father's arm around her waist; a Virginian with a mustache and a broad-brimmed soft hat who is determined to know "what Harrison is saying about his South." Harrison is drinking something brought to him in a deep cup so that people will think it is bouillon. He puts on his steel-framed spectacles and without hearing any cries of impatience from the crowds lost in that vast fog, without one man surrendering his place in that frigid mass of people, the President reads his inaugural address rapidly beneath an umbrella which a handsome man holds over his head as he stands upon a chair.

He begins reverently, addressing God and the nation. "It was a hundred years ago today," he says with sovereign and modest joy, "that the executive power of the United States began to function, that President George Washington took his oath of office. Before any other, we celebrate the centenary of the legislative power, from which all other power springs; our second century will not truly begin until we solemnize the first hundred years of the judicial power, which crowns them all. One of today's territories is larger than five States in those days! Let us thank God for this high point of glory, because our people are better clothed, eat better, and have better houses; because we have more teaching methods and teach more than before; because the sweet offices of charity have increased to keep pace with misfortune; because religion is growing and becoming stronger." There are sentences such as this: "What the body of the nation was a century ago, has become the hem of the national garment," a phrase for the West! Some ideas are worthy of being engraved.

"The only way to defend a country's independence is for each of its children to know how to become independent," a phrase against the office seekers! There are some rhetorical phrases of a novice: "Will the preoccupations and paralysis of slavery continue hanging from the cloak of progress?" He is straightforward and does not hide the sword. We can see his sword belt under his vest. He turns to the right and says to the rich: "Beware!" He turns to the left and says: "Beware!" to the poor. His foreign policy clearly states, "Beware!" The South must not come to the North to seek aid against the Negroes, because anyone who contracts "just obligations"—the obligation to be patient with the man he vilified and abused—must not ask another to pay his debts, "nor has anyone who denies the use of the law to others the right to solicit its protection for himself"—a doubly powerful phrase for other southern Democrats accused of stifling the Negro's Republican vote and robbing him of it![17] He freezes the bones of monopolies that demand official protection against the organized workers by asking this question, an admirable one: "If the educated and influential classes of a community practice or favor a systematic violation of laws which they believe opposed to their interests, what can they expect when the ignorant classes learn the lesson that the expedience of supposed interests of a class is a sufficient reason to violate those laws?" This entire paragraph is a golden one, like that which counsels careful consideration of the immigration coming to this country, and "that the utmost attention should be paid to the character and good disposition of the immigrants, even those of the best races, before giving them the right to be a burden to the Treasury, or disturb the social order, with their citizenship." "So great are the rights of the American citizen, and so solemn his duties that, before granting a foreigner his naturalization, we must know full well who he is, and be sure that he

17. After the Democrats returned to power in the South and with the final removal of the federal troops from the South by President Hayes, violence was used regularly as the surest means to keep Negroes from voting. Negroes were forced to become both politically impotent and economically subservient. Raids on Negroes by night riders such as the Ku Klux Klan, White Caps, Red Shirts Brigades, were used to prevent the Negro from voting. Later, in the 1890s, disfranchisement of Negroes was achieved legally with the passage of laws in the South specifically designed to rob Negroes of their vote. By the end of the 1890s, despite the Fifteenth Amendment to the Constitution which supposedly guaranteed Negro males the right to vote, the Negro was virtually disfranchised throughout the South. The Republicans protested but did nothing to reverse this tragic process.

knows and respects the rights he demands of us!" Here is what he says to Europe: "We have reason to hope that American policy in Europe—not meddling in foreign affairs—will be European policy in America... that no friendly government attempt to dominate the Canal that shortens the distance between our Atlantic and Pacific States... that no European government try to establish in the free countries of America the colonies which out of a sense of justice the American government does not try to establish." "Nor shall we insult any friendly flags or have our own flag or the rights of our citizens be insulted in continental lands or in the islands"—a phrase for Germany with regard to Samoa! "The courage and ability of our sailors have often in our extraordinary history given power to timid ships and to short-range cannons; they would do the same again, of this I have no doubt, but it is unfair to expose them, through negligence or lack of foresight, to unequal combat!" "And we must help in establishing new steamship lines, for as long as there are none, any increase of trade with other countries south of us is impossible!" This is how he treats the office seekers—a stain upon the nation and a plague upon life, at the same time as they are a source of power for any President: "Honest service to the party certainly will not be viewed by me as an obstacle to an attempt to obtain a public office," and he adds, fearful in the extreme because at the very door to his room this morning an office seekor assaulted him: "But inopportune insistance will not be the best way to obtain employment in the administration." This is his comment upon the Treasury: "Wastefulness, carelessness, and favoritism in national expenditures are criminal; the surplus must be reduced without investing it in unnecessary enterprises, or taking one atom away from our protective tariff, one article from the protection of our industries." That is how the message progresses, by considering the manifestation of the wrongs rather than their causes, by making judgments for the upper classes and granting the lower classes their rights to them. The President believes in classes: he sees them in life and talks about them in his address; he considers fostering them less dangerous than hindering them.

The important points of his address are the following: the southern Democrat must permit the Negro—the Republican Negro—to vote freely; immigration must be restricted, for it endangers us and brings us foreign ideas; articles made abroad must be prevented from being sold in the United States at less cost than those made in America, and American trade must be extended throughout the world; all posts that the law allows to hand out freely will be given to Republicans; the Navy must be enlarged as rapidly as perfection in work will permit, and it must be known that we are ready to fly our flag wherever another may attempt to be flown. He is distressed by what he sees in his own party and in the opposing one—mortal enmities, women's hatreds, blind jealousies, frantic interests which prefer anything to a rival's victory. And the general who is afraid of politics appears in this sentence: "Let those who know how to die upon the battlefield give a better proof of their patriotism and a higher glory to their country, furthering brotherhood and justice in their hearts!" The politician appears in this one: "A party's success by illegitimate means or by revolutionary practices is regrettable and transitory, even when viewed without considering anything but party interests."

And thus ends the discourse, acclaimed by hurrahs, an affectionate smile from Cleveland, a hundred hands held high from beneath umbrellas by people fighting to be the first to approach him, hats being waved by the dispersing multitude eager to take part in the parade, and music and cannon blasts. "No nation in the world has a government so worthy of respect and love, nor such vast and magnificent dominions so beautiful to see or so full of enterprise and work. God has placed a diadem upon our nation's head, and incalculable power and wealth beyond description at our feet. But we must not forget that we receive these gifts on condition that justice and mercy hold the reins of power, and that the avenues of hope are accessible to the entire nation!" Harrison and Cleveland, Morton and his attendants, climb into their landaus between walls of humans whom the shoulders of the police are unable to control; one landau is drawn by four sorrel horses, the other by four bays. The mounted police break into a gallop to clear the way. Sidewalks, railings, everything is filled with men, women, and children waving their handkerchiefs and umbrellas and shouting "God bless you!" The southern Negroes wave their torn hats, the northern Republicans their new derbies, and the shouting is continuous. One man, hanging from a window by his hands, asks for "three cheers, three cheers and the tiger!" An office seeker, wearing a petition on his coat sleeve, struggles with the police like a wild beast because

146

the police will not let him hold on to the carriage. A sandwich, a little more bouillon in the White House, and Cleveland, in his coupé of a free man, drives to a better presidency, the home of a friend, to dine with his wife. Harrison, in a silk hat and fur overcoat, leaves with his retinue for the uncovered platform to review, for three hours of strong winds and cheering, the army regiments, the "patriots" who had asked for their posts, the State militia, the fifty thousand men who, because of their own desire and at their own cost or that of their political party, have come to add splendor—with the ingenuity and abandon of real people, people who make mistakes and succeed, people who are able to love—to a public function that raises in their own estimation all who witness it, through the estimation they feel for this man. The passing cavalry do not stand up in their stirrups; it is the man watching them pass by who stands in them! Few others besides members of his family surround the President upon that cold and muddy platform with its rows of empty chairs, the only people being those who physically wish to protect the proud general. And with him is his wife dressed in a suit of Yankee wool like his: wife and daughters sitting impatiently, or serving tea, serving the generals tea with their own hands. Oh, that stubborn rain lashing people's faces, a rain that soaks through overcoats and dulls the luster of the parade!

Beaver is in command, une leg missing! Following the aides-de-camp with their dismal plumage go the artillery batteries. That colonel salutes Harrison with his stump, and Harrison takes off his hat as he does when the flags pass by. The cheering is not so loud that it muffles the sound of the falling rain, or the whistling wind that twists the flags, or the tired feet sloshing through the mud. Hundreds, thousands go by with banners, eagles, pennants, ships made of flowers. Now the militia with their regulation capes and vigorous step; then the joyful and unruly young people, their closed umbrellas under their arms and their hats over their hearts, or with a formidable mastiff wearing a brass collar that reads "PROTECTION!" or stopping before the platform and engaging in military drills with their red, white, and blue umbrellas in place of guns; or singing their college songs, wearing a rooster for a badge and a broom in their buttonholes. The Negroes from Maryland march in their light overcoats. The Irish from New Jersey break ranks in the center, assemble by their leaders, whirl like propellers, and continue marching crosswise. The "youths" from Newark wear red and white lancers' helmets and silver spurs.

Buffalo Bill[18] captures all hearts with his flowing hair, kerchief around his neck, and yellow suit; he is mounted like a cowboy upon a small, rotund, lively Moorish horse given to Grant by the Sultan; the horse cuts, capers, bites the bit, bucks in opposition, kneels, and breaks into a gallop when the hero is applauded. Then comes Jonathan at the head of his club, brandishing a large hat— floppy and greenish-yellow like a herring—its plush brim pulled down to the eyes when on his head, the points of his collar up to the cheekbones, the coattails of his blue dress coat reaching to the back of the knees, the star-speckled vest reaching to his belt, the trousers baggy at the knees and just escaping the ground, the tongued boots aggressive, wrinkled, and pontifical. Now what remains of the parade goes by in the dark.

The humid sky in the distance is illuminated with a hazy splendor, as if above an enormous oven. The troops disperse. Carriages go back and forth. Mounted errand boys pass by, and in the lamplight we see them carrying bunches of flowers. It is because the colossal Pensions Building—with its three rows of wide windows, its chimney sending smoke up to the very clouds, and its eight columns supporting the gigantic vault with a two storey gallery at its feet—is opening its doors to the ten thousand eager visitors who have come from everywhere in the country to see the marvel—its ballroom covering an entire acre and filled with pennants, coats-of-arms, and laurel wreaths. They have come to see its Presidential room which is a mass of palms and roses; its musicians by the hundreds to whose rhythm bald senators dance the quadrille, joyful as if in a newfound youth; its dining hall where the only wine served is pure milk, and the only champagne, water; the President's triumphal entry, his wife on his arm, dressed in domestic-made silks, amid the crowds who draw aside for them, aided by the shoulders of two athletes, because "the President wants no policemen when he goes among his people."

18. William Frederick Cody (1846-1917), American scout, Indian fighter, and showman. He obtained his reputation as "Buffalo Bill" by killing some 4,000 buffaloes in eighteen months as a hunter for the Union Pacific Railroad.

Hanging from the ceiling on thousands of ribbons are the national colors, to be gathered up around the friendly nations' coats-of-arms, surmounted by an eagle, cover the balconies, float from individual flagpoles, are displayed upon the presiding chair covered with immortelles, upon men's lapels, upon satin breastbands, and upon women's breasts in corsages of red roses, white carnations, and blue violets. And above everything those eight columns supporting the vaulted ceiling. At that very hour a New York gilder was picking up the tools of his trade. He had worked throughout the night painting a new name in gold letters upon the glass door of Bangs, Tracy and MacVeagh's office: GROVER CLEVELAND, ATTORNEY.

JOSÉ MARTÍ

La Nación, Buenos Aires, April 16, 1889